POLICY PAPERS

NUMBER 33

IRAN'S CHALLENGE TO THE WEST:
HOW, WHEN, AND WHY

PATRICK CLAWSON

THE WASHINGTON INSTITUTE FOR NEAR EAST POLICY
WASHINGTON, D.C.

Library of Congress Cataloging-in-Publication Data

Clawson, Patrick.
     Iran's Challenge to the West: How, When, and Why/
Patrick Clawson.
        p. cm. — (Policy Papers ; no. 33)
        ISBN 0-944029-24-8: $11.95
        1. Iran—Foreign relations—1979- I. Title. II. Series: Policy
Papers (The Washington Institute for Near East Policy) : no. 33.
    DS318.83.C58   1993
     327.55—dc20   93-12300
                    CIP

Cover design by Jill Indyk

THE AUTHOR

Patrick L. Clawson wrote this Policy Paper while serving as a Fellow in Economics at The Washington Institute for Near East Policy. He is currently a senior fellow at the National Defense University's Institute for National Strategic Studies and the editor of *Orbis*. A former economist at the World Bank and the International Monetary Fund, he is the author of *Unaffordable Ambitions: Syria's Military Buildup and Economic Crisis* (The Washington Institute, 1989), and co-author, with Howard Rosen, of *The Economic Consequences of Peace for Israel, the Palestinians and Jordan* (The Washington Institute, 1991).

CONTENTS

ACKNOWLEDGEMENTS

This Policy Paper would not have been possible without the continuing stimulation of my colleagues during my stay at The Washington Institute. Barbi Weinberg, Martin Indyk, Rob Satloff, Michael Eisenstadt, Laurie Mylroie, Harvey Sicherman, and Shai Franklin were a constant source of new ideas and useful comments on drafts. Yehudah Mirsky and Matt Ahrens were all of that, as well as able polishers of a rough draft into a final text. My thanks also for the comments of Colonel David Smith (U.S. Army) of the National Defense University's Institute for National Strategic Studies and Daniel Pipes of the Foreign Policy Research Institute (FPRI), and the insights I gained from participation in a series of workshops organized by Geoffrey Kemp at the Carnegie Endowment for International Peace. I am grateful for research asistance that was ably provided at FPRI by Chris Bailey of the University of Pennsylvania, and Michael Rubin of Yale University. As always, the responsibility for any errors and shortcomings is fully my own.

PREFACE

The aftermath of the Gulf War and the inauguration of a new administration in Washington provide an indispensable opportunity to re-examine American policy toward the Persian Gulf region in general, and Iran in particular.

Iran has long sought a commanding role in the Persian Gulf. Today, its principal rival, Iraq, has been substantially weakened as a result of the Gulf War and UN-imposed sanctions. The dissolution of the Soviet Union has provided Iran with a number of potential arms sources, and has created a number of newly independent, predominantly Muslim countries susceptible to Iran's influence. These factors have left a power vacuum in the region which Iran hopes to fill.

Many Western analysts, convinced that the so-called "moderates" currently ruling Iran are more sympathetic to Western interests than the "radicals," have been willing to overlook ominous signs of Iranian rearmament, nuclear ambitions, and undiminished efforts to export its brand of radical Islamic fundamentalism. They have given little credence to warnings about Iran from Western allies in the region such as Egypt and Saudi Arabia.

In this Policy Paper, Patrick Clawson systematically examines the challenges that moderate-led Iran poses to the West, and explores several potential responses to the Iranian challenge. The term "moderate" as applied to Iranian politics, he argues, refers only to its domestic policy; with respect to foreign policy, the virulent anti-Westernism of the moderates may be more dangerous than any threat posed by the radicals. In reality, it is the moderates, not the radicals, who in recent years have launched a major program to rebuild the military (including a quest for nuclear arms), to disrupt the current Arab-Israeli peace talks, and to escalate threats to smaller neighbors in the Gulf and in Central Asia.

As the West becomes more alert to the need to take steps to restrain the new and dangerous international arms trade along with its ongoing concern to protect the free flow of Persian Gulf oil, attention must be paid to an expansionist Iran which is seeking both nuclear and conventional arms in ever-greater numbers. This analysis is a vital contribution to informed discussion and debate of an issue likely to loom larger in the near future.

Barbi Weinberg
President
February 1993

EXECUTIVE SUMMARY

The government of Islamic Iran has long been split between "radicals" and "moderates" on matters of economic and social policy. The principal changes instituted by the moderates after they came to power with the election of Hashemi Rafsanjani as President in 1989 have been a greater reliance on market forces in the economy, and some improvement with respect to the status of women and freedom of the press.

Notwithstanding their more benign designation (which stems from moderation in domestic policy not foreign policy), the "moderates" may pose a greater threat than the "radicals" to stability in the Gulf and to Western interests since they may be more capable of carrying out anti-Western foreign policy objectives. Both groups see basic divergences of interest between Islamic Iran and the West, and both want Islam to play a major role on the world scene, whereas the U.S. supports a world order which does not differentiate among nations on religious grounds. Moderate-led Islamic Iran is, and will remain, unalterably opposed to the Arab-Israeli peace process, will continue to support violent anti-Israel groups like Hezbollah in Lebanon and Hamas in the occupied territories, and will support Islamic fundamentalism throughout the Muslim world. Both moderates and radicals are prepared to use terrorism to advance their interests. Indeed, the moderates may be even more reliant on terrorism: more Iranian oppositionists abroad were killed in Rafsanjani's first three years than during the ten years of Khomeini's rule.

Although all Iranians take the Persian character of the Persian Gulf very seriously, there are important distinctions between the moderate and radical views—the moderates care more about oil fields while the radicals are more interested in Islamic holy places located in Saudi Arabia and Iraq. The moderates have married traditional Persian nationalism with fundamentalist Islam to justify its attempts to dominate the region. Both groups expect that the end of the Soviet Union will signal a return of the Persian sphere of influence to what they regard as its rightful borders of the last three millennia—the seven successor states of the USSR were under loose Iranian control two hundred years ago. Both groups have become angry with Turkey, primarily because they fear that Turkish aid for newly independent Azerbaijan may contribute to growing nationalism among Iran's twelve million ethnic Azeris.

Overall, the triumph of the moderates over the radicals within Iran has produced few if any advantages for the West; instead, it has raised some troubling possibilities. The moderates have created lofty expectations of future prosperity among Iranians. The economic reality in Iran portends a different outcome—per capita income in Iran was cut in half between the Revolution and Khomeini's death, and no government can restore income quickly to the level the Iranian public regards as normal. Despite their rhetoric, the moderates have not implemented the deep reforms necessary to foster an economic recovery. Instead, they have invested in inappropriate, state-sponsored heavy industry while ignoring entrepreneurial light industry.

The moderate-led military build-up represents the largest challenge to the West. After the Revolution, the radicals were suspicious of the regular military, and thus directed imported arms to the Revolutionary Guards instead of the army. Soon after Rafsanjani took power, Iran initiated a five-year $10 billion military build-up of a nature not easily reconciled with defensive intentions. Iran's build-up is meant to project power and to complicate U.S. naval operations. Iran could well become a nuclear nation in the 1990s, especially if it can increase strategic cooperation with Pakistan, a nation which hopes to secure Iran as a counter to India and can offer little in return besides its nuclear bomb.

Iran could well find itself by the end of the 1990s with a stagnant income, inflated expectations, a heavy debt, and a large military. In this scenario, Iranian leaders would have little hope of resolving their economic crisis (and the resulting crisis of legitimacy) without using military might to pressure their Gulf neighbors, who sit on top of some of the world's most valuable resources. This "son of Saddam" scenario would be the direct result of the moderates' emphasis on economics and their rebuilding of the military, two policies that the radicals would not follow as vigorously—hence, the paradox that the moderates may be more dangerous to Western interests than the radicals.

Iran may bide its time before challenging the West, in order to rearm while the U.S. trims its own forces. However, Tehran's behavior indicates that it feels this is a particularly propitious moment; this may be because of an upsurge of Islamic fervor and the disarray in the wake of the Soviet Union's dissolution and Iraq's defeat, while delay may be more dangerous because the Arab states of the Gulf may acquire more weapons and Israel may reach peace with its Arab neighbors. It would thus be an error to assume that there will be no major Iranian challenge in the short term.

Iran has shown ingenuity in challenging the West in unexpected ways that play to Tehran's strength, as shown by the mining of the Gulf during the Iran-Iraq War. The U.S. must be prepared for the possibility of Iranian-sponsored destabilization of regional governments, as well as for the militarily most challenging case of an Iranian-organized coalition that strikes out at either Turkey, an ally of the U.S., or at Saudi Arabia, a friend of the U.S.

U.S. policy towards Islamic Iran could take one of three basic paths:

Bringing Iran into the family of nations. This policy has been adopted by Japan and Europe in their determination to work with the current Iranian government to whatever extent possible. This policy is based on the assumption that economic moderation and prosperity will lead to eventual foreign policy moderation. So far, there is little evidence to support this assumption. Indeed, it could be argued that additional resources have permitted Iran to accelerate its rearmament, to step up its pressure on Gulf states, and to play a more active role in Middle Eastern politics from Algeria to Sudan to Lebanon. A similar policy towards Iraq in the mid-1980s resulted in Saddam Hussein's invasion of Kuwait on August 2, 1990.

Applying carrots and sticks. A nuanced policy of rewarding positive steps and penalizing negative actions would allow flexibility, while in setting out the parameters, the U.S. would define the principles underlying its differences with Islamic Iran. This could provide the public with an understandable rationale for what could otherwise be seen as cynical *realpolitik*. Unfortunately, a carrot-and-stick policy would suffer from four defects. First, as the Iran-contra debacle showed, foreign governments can exercise only limited influence on Iran. Second, years of venomous relations between Iran and the U.S. render a nuanced carrot-and-stick policy emotionally impossible for either country to accept. Third, potential carrots will be irrelevant if Iran can obtain the same elsewhere without any change in behavior; Europe and Japan have not agreed with the U.S. on how to identify the criteria Iran must meet before receiving certain rewards. Fourth, the criteria themselves will be hard to formulate, because Islamic Iran has demonstrated a remarkable talent for observing the letter of the law while violating its spirit.

Containment. To the extent that Washington's basic interests are incompatible with Tehran's drive to dominate Gulf oil, confront Turkey, gain access to the Pakistani bomb, and provide support for anti-Western terrorism, the best American response may be containment. Similar to the American containment policy toward the Soviet Union during the Cold War, this policy would entail setting clear markers to avoid military confrontation, demonstrating a willingness to use force if those markers are crossed, and hoping that the regime's internal problems will eventually cause it to implode. Economic weakness increases the chances for containment to succeed, as does the growing disillusionment of the Iranian people with rampant corruption and their continuing poverty. Ironically, it may be easier to secure European and Japanese cooperation in a coordinated approach to Iran if Washington pushes for the isolation of Iran, rather than a nuanced carrot-and-stick policy for rewarding moderate behavior.

INTRODUCTION

In the 1990s, U.S. policy towards the Persian Gulf has been dominated by continuing problems with Iraq and the strategic alliance with Saudi Arabia. But these two countries have historically been the weaker legs in the Gulf's strategic triangle; throughout most of the last century—and indeed over the last three millennia—the dominant power in the region has been Iran, with more than half the region's population and control of nearly half the Gulf's coastline.

Does this remain so in the post-Desert Storm Gulf? Has there been a balance of power, a power vacuum, or a resurgence of Iran as the regional superpower? And should the West be concerned, given that none of the Gulf's states share Western democratic values and that Iran's revolutionary fervor appears to be waning?

In answering these questions, this Policy Paper presents three major arguments about Iran's challenge to the West:

• **Why**:   Strong national and economic interests will likely bring Iran's moderates into conflict with the West. In important ways, the moderates are more dangerous enemies of the West than are the radicals, with whom they share a continuing commitment to an anti-Western fundamentalism.

• **When**:   It might seem that Iran poses little immediate threat—its forces will remain weak for several years, and Tehran has an incentive to wait until the U.S. reduces its forces while Iran rearms and rebuilds its economy. But Iran is acting more aggressively on a variety of fronts. It seems to think that now is the time to act because the U.S. is preoccupied, the

region's instability creates openings, and anti-Western
Muslim movements are strong.

  • **How:**   Several plausible scenarios exist in which Iran
and the West could come to blows. Iran has demonstrated an
ability to challenge the West in ingenious and unexpected
ways. The most dangerous situations would be presented by a
military alliance between Iran and some other regional
actor(s).

In evaluating developments in Iranian policy one must
attempt to look at the world through Tehran's eyes. While the
U.S. may hold the perspective that it is the only superpower left
and so its power has never been greater, Iranian leaders feel
the world is going their way. The end of communism is seen
not as a victory for the West but as a sign of the weakness of
Islam's enemies. Has it not brought fifty million Soviet
Muslims actively back into the fold? Has it not meant victory
for the upholders of religion in Afghanistan? Has it not
brought the prospect of Islamic rule in Europe—in Albania and
Bosnia-Herzegovina?

Meanwhile, Desert Storm, which has eliminated the main
threat to Iran in the Gulf, may have created an opportunity for
Iran to exercise influence over the largest Shi'ite community
outside of Iran and to gain access to some of Shi'ism's most
holy sites. At the same time, the Arab states on the southern
side of the Gulf have been unable to construct a permanent
coordinated force, leaving Iran free to pressure each separately.
The continuing inability to force Saddam Hussein to bend
keeps the U.S. preoccupied and so less able to deal with Iran.
The region has come to understand just how apt the name
Desert Storm actually was—American power may be
devastating in its effect, but, like a storm, it leaves the scene of
destruction quickly. Those who can weather the storm will be
able to resume business as usual once it has passed.

Tehran is not alone in its judgment that world events in
1990-92 benefited Iran. Many in Washington would agree
with Gerald Seib's judgment:

> To an uncanny degree, Iran has benefited from virtually all the
> cataclysmic events that have rocked the world in the last two
> years. Operation Desert Storm crippled its biggest enemy, Iraq.
> ... Then, just as Iran embarked on rearmament, the collapse of
> the Soviet Union and the Warsaw Pact opened up a vast new arms

bazaar in which cash-starved Soviet-bloc nations are eager to sell weapons cheaply. At the same time, the Soviet breakup... has given Tehran 'a bigger playpen to operate in' by handing autonomy to six Muslim-dominated former Soviet republics to Iran's north, says former Defense Secretary James Schlesinger.[1]

Thus, at a time when the West is preoccupied with what to do with Saddam Hussein, and with the Arab-Israeli peace process, Iran may be increasing its challenge to the West while complicating these other concerns in the process.

This paper seeks to examine the nature of this challenge, and proposes several courses of action that the West may take in response.

---

[1] Gerald Seib, "Iran is Re-Emerging as a Mideast Power As Iraqi Threat Fades," *Wall Street Journal*, March 18, 1992.

1 IRAN'S MODERATES: NO FRIENDS OF THE WEST

Ever since the Iranian Revolution of 1979, there have been Washington observers who have argued that the U.S. should cultivate better relations with the moderate elements said to be in ascendancy in the Islamic Republic. These observers claimed that a more friendly attitude towards the moderates was the best means to promote geo-strategic cooperation against common enemies (first the Soviet Union, then Iraq) and to secure release of hostages (first from the U.S. embassy in Tehran under President Carter, then from Lebanon under Presidents Reagan and Bush).

Enthusiasm for an opening to Iranian moderates swept the U.S. media after the Majlis (Iran's parliament) elections in the spring of 1992. The *New York Times* forecast, "[President Hashemi] Rafsanjani will have enough support to counter political rivals and carry out his policies of an opening to the West and liberalizing Iran's economy." The *Los Angeles Times* said, "[the] elections will almost certainly open a wedge in more than a decade of hostility with Washington and Europe." A *Boston Globe* correspondent argued in the *New Republic*, "It would be more far-sighted for the United States to encourage [Rafsanjani's] embryonic changes than to continue to pursue a policy of total ostracism towards Tehran."[1]

---

[1] *New York Times*, May 10, 1992; *Los Angeles Times*, April 16, 1992; and *The New Republic*, June 8, 1992.

Many arguments have been made against cultivating relations with Iranian moderates; indeed, many are made later in this paper. But on one important point, those who favor good relations with the moderates are correct. There is indeed a real, continuing division between two large groups of politicians in Islamic Iran—the so-called "moderates" and "radicals."[1] Furthermore, as argued below, the terms accurately portray the differences between the two groups on domestic policy, though they are not informative about disagreements on foreign policy, which are, in any case, narrower. Since Iranians, like most peoples, concentrate on domestic policy rather than on foreign affairs, it is not surprising that the terms they have adopted for their political camps reflect the differences on domestic policy.

The competition between the two groups of politicians is real. Islamic Iran is not a monolithic state like Iraq or Syria, in which criticism of the government is neither tolerated nor even possible. Instead, Iran has a vigorous political life, within the confines set by unconditional support for an active role for Islam and the clergy in public life. The newspapers are full of lively debate while the radio and television cover speeches critical of the government in the Majlis. Majlis elections can be bitterly contested, with some margins of victory razor thin; there have been many tight votes and rejections of executive-branch proposals in the Majlis.[2] The opposition has derailed some of the government's priority projects, such as the reform of labor laws. In short, Islamic Iran has enjoyed a system that is as open for public debate as any known before in Iran's history. Indeed, Iran's parliament has fair claim to being the second most powerful in the Muslim world after Turkey.

To be sure, Iranian politics is not divided along neat fissure lines between two camps defined by ideology. Many political battles take place along lines, some of which have little to do with ideology, but with issues such as regional differences and the division of patronage. That said, the history of Iran since

---

[1] The terms "tundro" (radical) and "mianehro" (moderate) are used by ordinary Iranians to describe the two groups.

[2] Iran's Majlis has in fourteen years rejected more nominees for Cabinet positions than the U.S. Senate in over two hundred years.

the consolidation of clerical control in 1981 (and the exclusion of the remaining liberals who had participated in the Revolution in 1979 in conjunction with the clerics) has been largely the history of a struggle between two major camps, each of which has evolved over time.

IRANIAN POLITICS SINCE THE REVOLUTION

The shape of the power struggle has changed over the years. In the early 1980s, the main conflict was between activist radicals and the socially conservative traditionalists, some of whom had been associated with the Hojjatieh Society, an anti-Bahai organization banned under the Shah and later banned by Ayatollah Ruhollah Khomeini because it was considered divisive. The traditionalists differed with the radicals on a variety of issues, but most deeply on the active state role in the economy promoted by the radicals. The traditionalists were able to block government actions through their control of the Council of Guardians, a panel of senior clerics who have to certify legislation as being consistent with Islam.

Starting in the mid-1980s, the main line of dispute shifted to technocrats versus radicals. Correspondingly, the field of battle changed. The radicals lost control over the presidency with the election of Ayatollah Seyed Ali Khamenei; they also could not count on the support of Majlis Speaker Rafsanjani, whose main role was to put together compromises but whose sympathy was clearly more with the moderates. Nevertheless, the radicals retained control over the ministries, thanks to their strong backing from Prime Minister Mir Hossain Mussavi, as well as their predominant voice in the Majlis. Khomeini periodically issued delphic statements supporting one side or the other, but he largely confined himself to insisting that the two sides work together while, at the same time, respecting his wishes on basic points, especially continuing the war with Iraq and opposing Western culture and influence.

The power of the radicals had been eroding for a long time, when the moderates were finally able to consolidate their own power with the election of Rafsanjani as President in July

1989.[1] Rafsanjani had used his position as speaker of the Majlis to orchestrate a revision of the constitution reinforcing the powers of the president, including vesting that office with all the responsibilities previously held by the prime minister, a post which was later abandoned altogether.[2] Rafsanjani then ran for the presidency with only token opposition and with clear backing from Khomeini, given shortly before the latter's death in June 1989. Since 1989, Rafsanjani has steadily reinforced the moderates' control over the government apparatus, removing radicals from cabinet posts and then easing them out of the key bureaucratic posts. He has marginalized the institutions which radicals had formerly used as their strongholds and/or maneuvered the radicals out of those institutions. For instance, the host of revolutionary "foundations," created to handle property confiscated from followers of the Shah and then converted into a parallel government by-passing the technocrats, have had their privileges clipped and their top personnel replaced by moderates.

Contrary to journalistic reports, the April/May 1992 Majlis elections did not represent an important turning point. Many Western reporters suggested that Rafsanjani would finally be able to break free from the radicals once he secured a solid majority in the Majlis, whereas in fact there were no significant reforms that had been held back during the period from 1989 to 1992 by the Majlis. The Third Majlis (1988-92) was a forum for complaints, but it did not prevent Rafsanjani from implementing his basic program of economic reform. Whereas about a third of the 270 Majlis members supported him all the time, and another third opposed him consistently Rafsanjani was able to build coalitions that attracted the remaining undecided third, the 'waverers.' Rafsanjani had thus been able to get the Third Majlis to approve many of his reform measures. The Second Majlis had entertained a vigorous debate over the propriety of borrowing any money

---

[1] Prime Minister Mussavi had submitted a letter of resignation in September 1988, to protest the trimming of his powers. Khomeini did not accept Mussavi's resignation.

[2] The constitutional revisions were approved by referendum on July 28, 1989, the same day Rafsanjani was elected President.

abroad, at a time when Iran's reserves were at a record low and it badly needed to borrow money to acquire arms for fighting Iraq; by contrast, the Third Majlis approved the borrowing of $27 billion from foreign sources in the Five Year Plan in 1990. To be sure, the Majlis spent five months debating the plan in committee or on the floor, and many changes were made to the draft presented by President Rafsanjani. But the changes were in the underlying economic projections and in particular projects, not in the main outlines of the policies.

The vote in spring 1992 did not demonstrate that there had been much change in the public mood from the previous Majlis election in 1988 either. In the 1988 election, the vote was rigged by the Interior Ministry which was controlled by radicals and headed by Ali Akbar Mohtashemipur, who had earlier been involved in the bombing of the U.S. Marine Corps barracks in Beirut.[1] The voting in the 1992 election was rigged by the Council of Guardians, which was controlled by pro-Rafsanjani traditionalists. Rafsanjani manipulated the rules blatantly to achieve the results he wanted in the Majlis: candidates were required to pass an unconstitutional and obviously political test of qualifications, and candidates who passed the test were given exactly five days in which to campaign. It was hardly surprising therefore when the results favored those who had worked with Rafsanjani.

To be sure, the most radical elements in Iran still have powerful influence. Some of the revolutionary foundations, the Revolutionary Guards, the police-like local committees, and several other security organizations are controlled by aggressive revolutionaries either directly or through supporters in key positions who ignore presidential directives they dislike. And Ayatollah Khamenei, the official religious leader, has played to the radical crowd in sermons (especially since summer 1992), in part to express his dissatisfaction at being

---

[1] Mohsen Rafiqdoust, the Revolutionary Guard Minister, admitted that Iran had trained the individual who had carried out the bombing. The bomb itself came to Lebanon via Syria where Mohtashemipur was Iran's ambassador. Robin Wright, *In the Name of God: The Khomeini Decade* (New York: Simon & Schuster, 1989), pp. 120-123.

side-lined by Rafsanjani.[1] But the trend of increasing moderate power is clear; the radicals openly admit that their day is past.

DIFFERENCES BETWEEN RADICALS AND MODERATES

The major differences between Iran's radicals and moderates have always been over domestic policy. In part that is because of the universal principle that "all politics are local politics": in other words, foreign policy often takes a back seat to domestic issues in Iran as elsewhere. In addition, there have not been profound differences over foreign policy. Consider, for instance, the issue of relations with the U.S. Clearly there are differences between the two camps, but the range is not large. The radicals oppose all public official contacts with the U.S. or indeed anything resembling such contact; ergo they berated Iran's UN ambassador for attending a Council on Foreign Relations seminar in summer 1992. The moderates at their most daring propose occasional official contacts, which is not exactly a pro-U.S. position.[2] Furthermore, the reality is that radicals themselves are prepared to talk to U.S. officials behind closed doors, as was shown during the Iran-contra affair.

Two areas in particular have stood out in the disputes between radicals and moderates: social/cultural policy and economic policy. On the social/cultural front, the radicals believe in state-imposed Islamic morality, including rigid enforcement of dress restrictions (women may neither show

---

[1] Khamenei gave a series of sermons on the propagation of virtue and condemnation of vice in which he extolled radical Hezbollah elements: "Let us not think that a Hezbollah is a young man who is rowdy, loud, and illiterate... The presence of Hezbollah elements must be foremost in many places." *Foreign Broadcast Information Service: Near East and South Asia*-92-147 [hereinafter cited as *FBIS-NES*], July 30, 1992, p. 37; see also *FBIS-NES*-92-135, July 14, 1992, pp. 48-50. The origins of the tensions between Khamenei and Rafsanjani are well analyzed by Nora Boustany, *Washington Post*, October 19, 1992.

[2] Robin Wright, "Iranian Leader Hints at Better Ties with U.S.," *Los Angeles Times*, February 1, 1993, reports that Iran called off a planned meeting of U.S. and Iranian UN ambassadors set for October 1992 when Tehran concluded that President Bush would probably lose the upcoming American elections.

hair nor wear any makeup in public) and banning of Western culture (some go as far as seeking to ban all musical instruments, while almost all radicals oppose the public use of the Roman alphabet in signs and advertising). The moderates feel that the government should encourage such admirable rejection of Western values while enforcing a more minimal standard. Intriguingly, some of the socially conservative senior clergy prefer the moderate stance on this point, because their tradition has been that Islamic mores should be enforced by social pressure rather than government action—they agree with the radicals on what constitutes Islamic morality, but, unlike the radicals, they want the community, rather than the state, to enforce such standards. Thus they approve of the roving gangs on motorcycles that periodically harass women with bad *hejab* (a term that has come to mean modesty and simplicity in dress, not just covering hair), while radicals would prefer enforcement of *hejab* by government-organized vigilantes (the *komiteh*s).

On the economic front, the radicals want to install a system of Third World socialism similar to that of India or Nasserist Egypt with self-sufficiency, income redistribution, and a state controlled-economy as its guiding principles. Policies intended to implement these principles include extensive price controls, a government-run foreign trade monopoly, publicly-sponsored distribution centers to control most wholesale trade, a rigid exchange rate (despite raging inflation that undermines the value of the currency), priority to government-owned heavy industry for credit and imports, promotion of import substitution rather than of exports, administrative measures to promote agriculture, and de-emphasis of the oil industry.

The radical agenda has little to do with Islam as traditionally interpreted, and much to do with Third World radicalism. The radical condemnation of merchants and promotion of direct distributive cooperatives has few roots in Islam, a religion that was founded by a merchant and which has long been friendly to trade. Indeed, on some points where the Koran lays out specific economic injunctions, radicals have acted contrary to the spirit if not the actual letter of the Koran. For instance, the Koran identifies certain taxes and condemns any introduction of other levies, yet the radicals want much higher taxation levels (the Koranic limits are admittedly unrealistic for modern societies, unless they have levels of oil income on a par with Saudi Arabia). The traditional religious leaders were outraged, and some senior ayatollahs called for a boycott of anti-Islamic taxes. Nor is this an isolated example. Time and again during the radicals' heyday in the early 1980s, their policy initiatives would pass the Majlis only to be blocked by the Council of Guardians, which must certify all legislation as consistent with Islam and the constitution.

As part of the Third World radical economic approach, the radicals were more interested in justice than in growth. Ali Mohtashemipur, perhaps the leading radical, made opposition to economic reform and to the priority given to economic growth the main issue during his successful 1989 run for Majlis.[1] In *Salaam*, a newspaper that frequently presents the radical viewpoint, 1992 Majlis candidate Fakhreddin Hejazi explained the radical economic program:

> We are opposed to trade without the Islamic government's control... If the curb on the private sector is lifted we will have neither bread nor religion... The economy of an Islamic country must be regulated in such a way that there will be neither poor nor rich people... Should we relax and eat [imported and relatively expensive] bananas? Do you know how much they cost? It is breaking the backs of thousands of downtrodden carpet weavers and ruining their lives.[2]

The moderates want to return to the economic policies of the Shah. The guiding principles are maximizing oil income to generate the resources to industrialize the country in a private-government partnership. The implementing policies are outlined in the Plan and Budget Organization's proposed 1993-97 Plan: "promotion of competition" ("the existing monopolies ... shall be abolished"), a market-determined exchange rate (a floating rate with "cancellation of restrictions on exchange buying and selling"), "transfer of all industrial

---

[1] He gave a long interview to *Khorassan*, printed in *Akhbaar*, September 24, 1990, centering his views about the Rafsanjani government's economic policies.

[2] *Salaam*, April 8, 1992, as printed in *Akhbaar*, April 8, 1992.

units [from the two government holding agencies] to the non-government sector," a balanced budget ("government borrowing from the Central Bank shall be equal to naught"), and other measures that could easily have been copied from a World Bank or IMF report.[1]

When Rafsanjani became president in July 1989, he turned his attention first and foremost to economic policy. In January 1990, Rafsanjani gained Majlis approval for a far-reaching Five Year Plan, which authorized $27 billion in foreign borrowing. This Majlis vote was followed with a series of reform measures, adopted in consultation with the IMF, that slashed the government budget deficit by more than two-thirds between 1988-89 and 1990-91,[2] opened up the economy to freer trade by removing most of the red tape blocking imports, and expanded the use of the free market exchange rate (then, as now, about 1,400 rials per dollar) instead of the "official" rate of about seventy rials per dollar. The Tehran stock exchange was revived in late 1990, with the privatization of thirteen government-owned firms whose shares were sold on the exchange.[3] The government ceased distributing 900 of the 960 commodities it had distributed previously.[4] The results of the Rafsanjani reform program have been dramatic.[5] Iran's imports rose from $11 billion in 1980-89 to $25 billion in 1991-92. Iran secured nearly $7 billion in foreign loans in 1990-91. Foreign investors are financing most of a $2 billion aluminum smelting complex, now under construction. Spurred by a jump in investment, Iran's economy took off— real GDP grew by 25

---

[1] *Resalat*, October 25, 1992, as printed in *Akhbaar*, October 25 and 27, 1992.

[2] International Monetary Fund, *International Financial Statistics*, shows the deficit in 1988-89 as 2.10 trillion rials and in 1990-91 as .66 trillion rials.

[3] *Bayan* as printed in *Akhbaar*, December 18, 1990.

[4] *Keyhan*, August 27, 1990.

[5] For a general evaluation of the reform program, see Vahe Petrossian, "Rafsanjani's Reform Dilemma," *Middle East Economic Digest* [hereinafter cited as *MEED*], April 24, 1992.

percent from 1989-90 to 1991-92. In short, Iran has been in the midst of a boom since 1989-90.

In addition to economic policy, the other major area of difference between moderates and radicals has been social policy. The most important social issue has been the role of women in society. For years, the best indication of who was ahead in the power struggle between moderates and radicals was the vigor with which rules restricting Western and other forms of "immodest" dress were enforced.

The issue at stake should not be seen as purely one of religion versus secularism, for the conflict was also one of urban sophistication versus rustic tradition. Often, the radicals objected to aspects of modernity which had little if anything which could offend religious principles. Take for example the controversy over the April 1992 replacement of the 1979 national anthem. The old anthem had been "a three-minute-long cacophony of village chanting—full of fervor but lacking melody [which] could have been sung by anarchic village boys and was an embarrassment to sophisticated city folk."[1] The new anthem, which is two minutes shorter, is sung by a mixed chorus of men and women backed by a Western-style orchestra—anathema to radicals who, in the early days of the Revolution, sought to ban from the radio both mixed choruses and musical instruments, preferring the unaccompanied male voice. Another step which displeased both the traditionally-educated and the radicals while pleasing the Western-educated and the moderates was the replacement of revolutionary slogans with commercial billboards, most advertising Western goods. Ayatollah Ahmad Jannati, head of the Islamic Propagation Organization and secretary of the Council of Constitutional Guardians, complained that the Revolution had "turned pale."

Changes in social policy in 1992 caused a reaction late in the year. Islamic Guidance Minister Khatemi had to resign after a series of controversies caused by the radical outcry over some of the liberalization measures he permitted, such as the airing of the first major U.S. movie (*Dances with Wolves*) since the Revolution. The moderates' social policy is likely to remain more contentious than economic reform, in part

---

[1] Vahe Petrossian, *MEED Iran Quarterly Report*, June 1992, pp. 11-12.

because during his drive to consolidate power, Rafsanjani made an alliance with a group of free market but socially conservative clerics who now form an important bloc in the Majlis more or less led by Ayatollah Azeri Qomi.

Nevertheless, the triumph of the moderates after Rafsanjani became president made a clear difference in both economic and social policy. Has it meant a similar change in foreign policy, away from aggressive rhetoric and destabilization of moderate regimes? Quite the contrary. The most dangerous aspect of the old foreign policy—an anti-Western concept of Islam—has remained, and has been joined by new elements that threaten Western interests.

ANTI-WESTERN CONCEPT OF ISLAM

Under Rafsanjani, the leaders of the Islamic Republic remain committed to a world-view in which the West, as led by the U.S., is the main enemy of Islam and, therefore, of Iran. In July, 1992, Ayatollah Ali Hosein Khamenei, leader (*faqih*) of the Islamic Republic, gave a series of addresses "on the propagation of virtue and combating vice" in which he restated the basic anti-Western theme:

> Today, just like in recent years, the fundamental enmity, the huge assault, the basic danger, come from world domination... Of course, the tyrannical and aggressive U.S. government is the leader... We must not make a mistake in recognizing the enemy. We must not believe for one minute that the enemy has stopped in its enmity against Islam and the Muslims.[1]

On many key foreign policy issues, the Iranian moderates are as committed as the radicals to anti-Western actions:

• *Opposition to the existence of Israel.* The moderate-controlled Foreign Ministry was behind extreme statements about Muslims everywhere having a responsibility to block the Arab-Israeli peace talks; it also lobbied the Islamic Conference Organization at its meeting in Dakar in December 1991 to call for a *jihad* (holy war) against Israel. At the International Conference for the Support of the Muslim Palestinian People's

---

[1] Voice of the Islamic Republic of Iran [hereinafter cited as VIRI], July 29, 1992, as printed in *FBIS-NES*-92-147, July 30, 1992, p. 35.

Revolution, held in Tehran on October 19-22, 1991, Iran reportedly offered $2 million per month to organizations to declare their opposition to negotiations.[1] The 1992-93 foreign exchange budget includes, under the President's $180 million special fund, $20 million for Aid to the Palestinian Islamic Revolution.[2]

Iran worked hard to sabotage the Arab-Israeli peace talks during 1992. They stirred up trouble in southern Lebanon before the June 1992 Israeli elections. The *New York Times* wrote at that time, "Some officials believe Iran through its surrogates in Lebanon tried to engineer a war between Syria and Israel to sabotage the Middle East peace talks."[3] In early October 1992, the Rafsanjani government invited delegations from Lebanese Hezbollah and the Palestinian Hamas to Tehran. The Hamas delegation was led by Dr. Mousa Abu-Marzuk who lives in Falls Church, Virginia. During their visit, which was front-page news in Tehran, they met with President Rafsanjani, Foreign Minister Velayati, Majlis Speaker Nateq-Noori, and Ayatollah Khamenei. At the end of the meeting with Khamenei on October 5, he "ordered, 'As Muslims, we ... will not let slip any opportunity to support the Islamic revolt of the Palestinian people.'"[4] On October 11, Hezbollah Secretary General Sayed Hassan Nasrollah explained to Rafsanjani "the glorious operations mounted by the Lebanese militants against the occupier Zionist regime."[5] Israeli sources indicate that soon thereafter Iran shipped to Hezbollah (via Syria) anti-tank and anti-aircraft weapons more sophisticated than any they had previously owned.

Armed and encouraged, Hezbollah initiated a campaign of shelling Israel, designed to provoke the outbreak of general warfare and to derail the peace talks. On October 25, a

---

[1] Safa Haeri, *Middle East Insight*, October 25, 1991, p. 12.

[2] *Resalat*, April 15, 1992 as printed in *Akhbaar*, April 15, 1992.

[3] Elaine Sciolino, *New York Times*, June 7, 1992.

[4] *Keyhan*, October 6, 1992.

[5] Tehran Radio, as printed in *Akhbaar*, October 11, 1992.

Hezbollah bomb killed five Israeli soldiers in southern Lebanon; a senior U.S. official was quoted in the *Los Angeles Times* laying the responsibility directly at the feet of Iran.[1] Israel mobilized forces for a large-scale action in Lebanon, and the continuation of the peace talks appeared to be in jeopardy. Fortunately, Hezbollah did not sustain its attacks. The lesson of this episode is that, with Syrian approval, Iran can endanger the peace talks via low risk support for the most hard-line rejectionists.

During the October meetings, Iran agreed to allow the Palestinian radical organization Hamas to open an embassy in Tehran and agreed to help train fighters and provide $15 million in funding per year for two years.[2] Accepting Iranian support forced Hamas to change its past attitudes: Hamas had long been cool towards Iran because of traditional antagonism between Shi'ites and the Muslim Brotherhood, the fundamentalist organization from which Hamas was formed.[3] It is too early to know how great a role Iranian support has played in Hamas' decision to launch an armed struggle, a step that has endangered its above-ground network that has been active in mosques, schools, and community organizations. Hamas has claimed responsibility for the murder of eight Israeli soldiers (five Jews and three Arabs) in December 1992 and January 1993. It seems plausible that Hamas would have been influenced by the increased support from a state sponsor that was able to provide funds, encouragement, training camps, a base from which leaders could operate openly, and a safe haven when needed.

---

[1] *Los Angeles Times*, October 30, 1992.

[2] See the Israeli magazine *Monitin* and the lengthy history of Hamas in *al-Wasat* magazine, as printed in *FBIS-NES*-92-236, December 8, 1992, p. 10.

[3] The distance between Iran and Hamas had eroded, in part because Hamas leaders expelled by Israel from the Gaza Strip, once Jordan refused to accept them, were released in the area of southern Lebanon controlled by the Iranian-backed Hezbollah. The exiled Hamas leaders were forced to turn to Hezbollah for support, which gradually brought Hamas closer to Hezbollah's patron, Iran.

Support for the most hard-line, anti-PLO and anti-Israel forces is a policy that has been endorsed just as much by Iran's moderates as by the radicals. The archetypal moderate, Foreign Minister Velayati, in an interview with *ad-Dastur* (Amman), said that

> We believe that the well-being of the Muslim states is achieved by being aware of and ready to confront the Israeli attempts to achieve such objectives [its expansionist intentions and continued aggression against Muslim states to control their strategic resources], and warning against optimism over the results of talks with such an enemy.[1]

In the summer of 1992 moderates quickly denied reports that Iran would reopen diplomatic relations with Egypt. While ties had been broken in 1979 when Egypt gave refuge to the Shah, the issue was barely mentioned in the Iranian press campaign. Instead, the Egyptian government was castigated for its willingness to make peace with Israel. Mohammad Javad Larijani, the current chair of the Majlis Foreign Relations Committee who had to resign his post in the Foreign Ministry in 1989 after writing about the possibility of resuming an Iranian-U.S. dialogue, felt that nothing good could come from relations with Egypt because, "The Zionist regime fears a day when Moslems will be able to establish legitimate Islamic governments in Egypt, Jordan, and other regional countries... The incumbent Egyptian regime does not fall behind the Zionists in any respect when it comes to animosity towards Islam."[2]

• *Intolerance for Christian minorities in Muslim states.* Iran has aided Sudan in its anti-Christian campaign. Rafsanjani visited Khartoum in December 1991 to applaud Sudanese religious intolerance and offer financial and material support for the war in the South. Justin Arop, who represents the Sudanese People's Liberation Army in Nairobi, said Iran had sent at least

---

[1] *Ad-Dastur*, June 22, 1992, as printed in *FBIS-NES*-92-121, June 23, 1992, p. 59.

[2] Larijani's regular weekly column in *Ettela'at*, July 23, 1992, as printed in *Akhbaar*, July 23, 1992.

2,000 soldiers and military advisors to Sudan.[1] To be sure, the Sudanese opposition has an incentive to exaggerate the extent of the Iranian role and makes some clearly implausible statements, such as the Cairo-based National Democratic Rally claim that 18,000 Iranian troops were in the South with combat planes, tanks, and artillery.[2] But there is good reason to believe that Iran funded the transfer from China of eighteen F-7 and F-8 fighter aircraft, 160 tanks, and multiple launch rocket systems, worth $300 million.[3]

• *Support for anti-government extremists in other Muslim countries.* Two popular members of the Jordanian parliament were convicted by a military court of accepting large sums from Iran to stir up anti-government sentiment. Youssef Ibrahim summarized the views being heard in much of the Arab world:

> In the past year, Algeria, Egypt, Tunisia and Jordan, as well as Israel and the Palestinian Liberation Organization, have battled militant fundamentalists... A senior Arab security officer in Amman, who like several others interviewed spoke on the condition of anonymity, described Iran's ambitions as a 'very big plan which we are all treating as an actual war being waged from Tehran.' Among other things, security officers report well over twenty ideological and military training camps in Sudan, Lebanon, and Iran are being run by Arabic-speaking Revolutionary Guards... The Foreign Ministry has a division to manage Arab fundamentalists. It is headed by the younger brother of President Hashemi Rafsanjani. The Revolutionary Guards handle military training in Sudan, Lebanon, and Iran...

---

[1] David Chazan, Agence France-Presse [hereinafter cited as AFP], March 26, 1992, as printed in *FBIS-NES*-92-061, March 30, 1992, p. 15.

[2] AFP, 21 February 1992, as printed in *FBIS-NES*-92-036, February 24, 1992, p. 27.

[3] *MEED*, March 6, 1992, p. 24. However, Sudanese Foreign Minister Ali Ahmad Sahlul has argued, "The Iranians present in Sudan do not exceed 88 in number... The weapons which Sudan obtained from Iran were limited in terms of quantity, and they were accompanied by big controversy over payment of their cost." *Al-Hayat* (London), May 16, 1992, as printed in *FBIS-NES*-92-098, May 20, 1992, p. 9.

> Some Arab experts say the scale of Iranian spending on the militancy is huge.[1]

The Egyptian government has adopted a shrill tone denouncing Iranian encouragement for terrorist attacks carried out by the loosely organized Islamic Society (*Gamaat*). After terrorists linked to the Islamic Society killed a British tourist and wounded four German tourists in fall 1992, Egyptian President Hosni Mubarak placed responsibility for the attacks on Iran: "[*Al-Ahram* editor Ibrahim] Nafei says that documents in the possession of the Egyptian security forces prove that the terrorists [who attacked foreign tourists] get their orders from Egyptians living in Iran. They went to Iran— some to Sudan—after the guerrilla camps in Afghanistan were closed."[2] To be sure, the Egyptian government has an incentive to exaggerate outside involvement, and some of the charges are overblown (e.g., Agriculture Minister Yousef Wali claimed that Iran is plotting to blow up the Aswan Dam).[3]

While it seems unlikely that 2,000 Iranian revolutionary guards are training Muslim extremists in Sudan for terrorist attacks in Egypt, as claimed by Egyptian Interior Minister Abdel-Halim Moussa,[4] there can be no doubt that Sudan's neighbors "are concerned about the destabilizing potential of a Khartoum-Tehran axis aimed at promoting Islamic governments."[5] There does seem to be a definite link between Iran and Islamists trained in Sudan. For example, Majid Kamal, an Iranian diplomat said to have been active in

---

[1] Youssef Ibrahim, "Arabs Raise a Nervous Cry over Iranian Militancy," *New York Times*, December 21, 1992.

[2] *Mideast Mirror*, November 19, 1992.

[3] *Economist*, November 28, 1992.

[4] *Washington Times*, December 3, 1992.

[5] Jennifer Parmelee, "Sudan Denies 'Khartoum-Tehran Axis' to Promote Islamic Regimes in Africa," *Washington Post*, March 12, 1992.

promoting Hezbollah while posted in Lebanon, has been in Khartoum for three years.[1]

Sudan is becoming increasingly economically dependent on Iran. Sudan's Finance and Economic Planning Minister Abdel-Rahman Hamdi and Energy and Mining Minister Othman Abdel-Wahab, during their January 1992 visit to Tehran, signed an agreement to buy 24,000 barrels of oil per day (1.2 million tons a year) in return for livestock and wheat, in a deal valued at $300 million a year.[2] During the visit of Sudan's Revolutionary Command Council for National Salvation Colonel Sulayman Muhammad Sulayman to Tehran in July 1992, it was announced, "a contract is expected to be signed between the two countries with Iran rendering technical assistance to Sudan for oil exploration," which may serve to revive plans to produce 200,000 b/d.[3]

Iran broke with its long-time ally Algeria in order to provide support, at least through propaganda, to Algeria's main fundamentalist group, the Islamic Salvation Front (known by its French acronym FIS). Tehran was also said to be aiding General Mohammed Farah Aideed in Somalia in early 1992, precisely at the time that the warlord launched his pillaging campaign that led to the starvation of tens of thousands of innocent civilians.[4]

• *Threats against Westerners perceived as anti-Muslim.* The most notorious case is that of Salman Rushdie, a British citizen whose life has been under continual threat from Iranian leaders for the last four years because his book, *The Satanic Verses,* allegedly blasphemes against Islam. Chief Justice of the Supreme Court Ayatollah Morteza Moqtada'i has confirmed

---

[1] Jennifer Parmelee, *Washington Post,* March 12, 1992.

[2] *MEED,* January 24, 1992, p. 22.

[3] Islamic Republic News Agency in English, July 28, 1992; *FBIS-NES-92-146,* July 29, 1992, p. 47. Chevron, which had begun to construct the oil pipeline and oil field facilities in Sudan before abandoning them as the war in the south reached the oil area and as the world oil market weakened, has not abandoned its claim and is not pleased at reports Iran may step in without compensation to Chevron.

[4] *Washington Post,* March 12, 1992.

that the death sentence is "an Islamic order and [is therefore] irrevocable."[1] There is no basis for the specious distinction drawn by Foreign Minister Velayati between a *fatwa* by Iran's religious leader and the Iranian government: Iran's constitution and its everyday practice both make clear that the government's actions are guided by the Supreme Jurist. Nor is the Rushdie affair the only case of inciting violence. Moderate President Rafsanjani urged Palestinians in May 1989 to "kill and execute—and not just inside Palestine—five Americans, or Britons or French" for every martyr of their own.[2]

• *Opportunistic use of terrorism.* Terrorism against Westerners continues under Rafsanjani's presidency. The last Western hostage in Lebanon was not released until December 1991, two years after Rafsanjani's election. The history of the hostages shows that despite its denials of responsibility, Iran was in control. If the Iranian government was not involved in the December 1988 downing of Pan Am 103 (Rafsanjani was, at the time, consolidating his position in a drive to take over the presidency six months later), it was not for lack of effort.[3] A "senior State Department official" told reporters there are "strong indications" that Iranian diplomats helped plan the March 1992 bombing of Israel's embassy in Buenos Aires in which 29 persons were killed.[4] The French weekly *L'Express* claims that Iranian agents were responsible for a grenade attack against the Istanbul synagogue on March 1, 1992 and the assassination of an Israeli security officer in Ankara a week later. It also claims that two Iranians about to carry out an assassination were caught red-handed in Paris in November 1992. It quotes an October 1992 report by the French security police (DGSE): "Through its political, logistical, and financial

---

[1] Islamic Republic News Agency [hereinafter cited as IRNA], as printed in *FBIS-NES*-92-219, November 12, 1992, p. 54.

[2] IRNA, May 5, 1989.

[3] Steven Emerson, *Washington Post*, November 17, 1991, summarizes the evidence that Syria and Iran targeted Pan Am planes and may have been involved in the downing of Pan Am 103.

[4] Alan Elsner, Reuters, May 8, 1992, as printed in *Washington Times*.

support, Iran continues to play a fundamental role in the development of Middle East terrorism."[1]

More recently, Iran has continued its support for terrorism within Turkey. An Iranian-backed group, Islamic Action, assassinated Ugur Mumcu, a popular Turkish investigative reporter and columnist with the left-leaning daily newspaper *Cumhuriyet* who was outspoken in his opposition to Islamic fundamentalism and Kurdish separatism, on January 25, 1993. The assassination prompted a virulent reaction—more than 100,000 people attended Mumcu's funeral, which became an anti-fundamentalist, pro-democracy rally. Protesters chanted anti-Iranian slogans: "Down with *sharia*. Down with Hezbollah. Mullahs to Iran. Turkey will never be Iran."[2] Four of the nineteen Islamic Action members who were arrested after the incident were Iranian. Turkish Interior Minister Ismet Szegin claimed that Mumcu's murder is linked to the murders of two other Turkish journalists, the kidnapping and murder of a member of the People's Mojahedeen (the Iranian opposition group), and the failed ambush of Jak Kamhi, a Turkish industrialist who is Jewish. Iran has allegedly provided sanctuary for three Islamic Action leaders, and has trained militants in military and assassination techniques in a camp in Iran. Turkish Prime Minister Suleyman Demirel said that although he did not want to "create problems between states," Turkey may be "facing incidents of Iranian origin."[3]

Moreover, there is ample reason to believe that Iran has recently organized the murders of several exiled Iranian opposition figures, despite the small threat their groups represent to the Islamic Republic. There is evidence that Iran was involved in the murder of former prime minister

---

[1] Xavier Raufer, "Tehran Persevere," *L'Express*, December 18, 1992.

[2] "Mumcu Funeral Turns into Anti-fundamentalist Protest as Demirel Wins Bagful of Gulf Cash," *Mideast Mirror*, January 27, 1993.

[3] "Demirel Does Not Rule out Iranian Involvement in Political Murders," *Mideast Mirror*, February 3, 1993. For more details on the various incidents, see Stephen Green, "Where Mideast Focus Should Shift," *Washington Times*, February 8, 1993, Alistair Lyon, "Turkey Says Murder Ring Had Iranian Links," Reuters, February 4, 1993, and *Mideast Mirror*, January 25, 26, 27, and 28, and February 3 and 4, 1993.

Shahpour Bakhtiar in August 1991 in Paris. The European Parliament has concluded, "There are some reasons to think that the assassination was committed by Iranian government agents."[1] While that may be a somewhat speculative conclusion, there is no doubt that the Iranian government has bitterly criticized and strongly pressured Switzerland for having the temerity to extradite to France one of the murderers for whom Iran claimed *ex post facto* diplomatic immunity.[2] The main defense of the Iranian terrorist was organized by the moderate-controlled Foreign Ministry, not by any radical-run revolutionary institution. At the same time that Iranian Foreign Minister Velayati assures Westerners that Iran's intentions are pacific, his ministry provides logistical support for terrorist operations. Either Velayati is dissembling or he lacks control over Iranian foreign policy; whatever the case, extreme caution is in order.

The assassinations of two successive leaders of the Iranian Democratic Party of Kurdistan provide another example of Iranian-organized murders of exiled Iranian opposition figures. On September 18, 1992, Sadegh Sharafkandi, leader of the Iranian Democratic Party of Kurdistan, and three companions were killed in Berlin, where they were attending the meeting of the Socialist International; his predecessor and two other party officials were killed in July 1989 in Vienna.[3] Of the five suspects arrested for the Berlin killings, the mastermind is said to have been the Iranian Kazem Darabi (his accomplices were Lebanese Shi'ites).[4]

THE MODERATES' ECONOMIC AGENDA

The anti-Western orientation of the radicals is clearly stronger than that of the moderates, for which reason Western

---

[1] Cited in *Iran Focus*, October 1991.

[2] To pressure Switzerland, Iran arrested a Swiss national on charges of illegal contacts with military personnel (*Financial Times*, March 31, 1992).

[3] *International Herald Tribune*, September 19, 1992.

[4] *Iran Times*, December 18, 1992; *L'Express*, December 18, 1992.

observers have long hoped that it would be easier to cooperate with the moderates. Unfortunately, other elements in the moderates' world-view will bring them into sharp conflict with the West. In particular, the moderates have promised the Iranian people a painless prosperity that will be possible only if Iran can somehow manage to dominate the Persian Gulf's oil supplies.

The moderates place great emphasis on economic growth, unlike the radicals who have been inspired by Khomeini's attitude that, "The people must make a decision: either comfort and an easy life or enduring hardships and safeguarding the country's independence."[1] That quintessential weather vane Khamenei echoed the same view while Khomeini's spirit was still strong: "The day, God forbid, that the Islamic Republic makes welfare and development its major objective and is ready to waive revolutionary ideals and forget the world message of the Revolution will be the day of degeneration and decline of all hope."[2]

On assuming the presidency, Rafsanjani lost no time in explicitly putting economic development as his top priority. In a series of sermons in fall 1989, he said:

> Thus far we in the cabinet have devoted the major part of our time to the issue of planning... The Koran says poverty is a source of shame in this world and in the next... The same sanctity we attach to the mosques and to praying, we should also show for economic issues.[3]

> Everyone should put on his overalls and walk on to the shopfloor and feel he is performing an act of worship just as in a mosque.[4]

---

[1] *Keyhan* (English), January 10, 1989.

[2] *Keyhan*, July 15, 1989.

[3] Tehran Radio, September 29, 1989, as printed in *FBIS-NES*-89-190, October 3, 1989.

[4] *Jomhuri Islami*, November 17, 1989, as printed in *Akhbaar*, November 18, 1989.

The moderates may be playing with fire by raising the expectations of Iranians to a level incompatible with Iran's own resources. To rest the legitimacy of the government on its ability to deliver economic growth is dangerous, because Iranians may remain profoundly discontented even if the government can deliver what most countries would consider excellent growth, say 3 percent to 4 percent per capita per annum. Iranians are likely to be ungrateful because they remember, or have heard about, the "golden days" under the Shah.

The popular perception that times are tough compared to what they were before 1979 is solidly grounded in fact. At the time of the debate about the Five Year Plan shortly after Rafsanjani became president, a flood of commentaries related the bitter truth about the Revolution's economic record. The Chamber of Commerce pointed out that per capita GDP, in 1974-75 prices, rose from 56,000 rials in 1968-69 to 112,000 in 1977-78 and then declined sharply to 54,000 in 1988-89[1]—quite a commentary on the Revolution. The sad truth is that under radical rule, Iran's per capita income halved. While the economy has grown under Rafsanjani, it remains well below its pre-revolutionary peak. In 1992-93, per capita income at 1974-75 prices is roughly 70,000 rials.[2]

These figures are hard to translate into dollars because the economy has been distorted by price controls and artificial exchange rates. One realistic estimate is that of the Iranian Central Bank Governor, who has referred to the 1991-92 GDP as $100 billion. That means per capita income is $1,650—less than in 1978-79 before adjustment for inflation, and of course much less after adjustment.[3] It is worth noting that within this

---

[1] *Akhbaar*, December 20, 1989.

[2] Unless otherwise noted, data on national income accounts and on the balance of payments comes from Central Bank of Iran (Bank Markazi Iran), *Annual Report*. The 1992-93 estimate is based on the government's projection of real growth for the year, which implies a GDP at 1974-75 prices of 4.1 trillion rials.

[3] Central Bank Governor Mohammed Hossein Aadeli, *Jomhuri Islami*, August 22, 1992. The GDP was 40 trillion rials, so the Governor was using an exchange rate of 400 rials per dollar. The World Bank, in its

general picture of declining income, the income of the modern-educated sectors has declined proportionately more, the poor have fared about the same as the average, and the traditionally-oriented have done better.[1]

The halving of national income was, in certain respects, not as serious a problem as the three-fourths drop in per capita foreign exchange earnings. An editorial in the most pro-business newspaper, *Resalat*, set forth Iran's fundamental economic problem since the Revolution, which is that export earnings dropped three-fourths:

> In 1977-78 the country had a population of 34.6 million and a foreign exchange revenue of $29.2 billion [i.e., $800 per person]... In the year ended March 20, 1992, our population was 60 million and our exchange earnings were only $15.7 billion... and the purchasing power of the dollar has dropped by at least 30 percent since 10 years ago [implying exports of $200 per person at 1977-78 prices].[2]

Insofar as Iranians judge the Rafsanjani government by its ability to restore the high incomes enjoyed between 1974 and 1978, they will remain discontented. There is no plausible way to recapture the 1979 levels within the next ten years. The great challenge for the Rafsanjani government will be to persuade Iranians that they should be content because their incomes, though lower than in the past, are rising. The task is not made easier by the intensive and successful propaganda that wrongly blamed Iran's economic problems on the "imposed war" with Iraq. The war has been over for four years, however, and, although the economic situation has improved, it has certainly not gone back to the pre-war level.

Iran's economic problems should not be ascribed solely to the Revolution and the war with Iraq that followed in its wake.

---

annual *World Development Report* for 1992, shows a per capita GNP of $2,450, which seems out of line with Iran's social indicators (literacy, access to health care, life expectancy, food consumption, and so on).

[1] Patrick Clawson and Vahid Nowshirvani, "The State and Social Equity in Post-Revolutionary Iran," in Myron Weiner and Ali Banuazizi, *The Politics of Social Transformation in Afghanistan, Iran and Pakistan* (Syracuse: Syracuse University Press, 1993).

[2] Ahmad Tavakoli, *Resalat*, August 16, 1992.

Islamic Iran was hit by the softness in world oil markets which reduced prices and limited the amounts that could be sold. Continued imperial rule would have made some difference since Iran might have exported higher volumes of oil, but that could have provoked steeper declines in world oil prices. Thus, it is not clear that continued rule by the Shah would have meant more oil income. Indeed, it is instructive to compare the economic problems that have beset Islamic Iran to those experienced by other OPEC members. On balance, Iran's economic situation has been about average for OPEC members. Its national income has not declined as steeply as that of Nigeria or Saudi Arabia; there have not been riots against economic discontent as extensive as those in Venezuela or Algeria. Nor has Iran been able to diversify to replace lost oil income as has Indonesia. Seen against the background of other OPEC nations—the most relevant comparable group—Islamic Iran's ability to diversify in order to compensate for lost oil income is mediocre.[1] Unfortunately for Iran's leaders, Iran's performance has not been able to match the people's expectations.

With sounder economic policy, Islamic Iran could have avoided much of the income decline it experienced in the 1980s. Iran was well positioned in 1979 for an economic take-off that would have reduced its dependence on oil income and left it less vulnerable to the subsequent softness in world oil markets.[2] It had improved its physical infrastructure, had a large pool of technically skilled laborers and experienced businessmen, and had a wide range of modern factories. Another plus for the post-revolutionary economy was that oil prices during the first three years were at their highest levels ever. All these advantages were canceled by inappropriate government policies. The revolutionary government systematically limited the role of market forces with a maze of regulations. Government finances were drained by a host of

---

[1] See Patrick Clawson, "Making the Best of Difficult Times: Economic Development in the Persian Gulf in the Face of Low Oil Income," *Iranian Journal of International Affairs*, Spring 1990.

[2] Jahangir Anuzegar, *The Dynamics of the Iranian Revolution* (Albany: State University of New York Press, 1991), pp. 53-66, evaluates Iran's economic circumstances and prospects in 1979 with an even hand.

subsidies, most of which were disguised through the use of artificially cheap imports. Much of the productive sector was transferred to the government and revolutionary foundations.

Whatever the evaluation of past economic performance, in the future the Rafsanjani government will be hard pressed to deliver any real increase in per capita income. The challenges can be grouped into two large categories—tremendous capital needs and few means to generate capital—each of which has several components.

Tremendous capital needs

• *Deteriorated capital stock from the war damage.* The official estimate presented to the UN showed direct damage from the Iran-Iraq War that the UN translated into $97.3 billion.[1] That estimate may have been too high, even though it excluded many of the elements claimed by Iranian propaganda about the war's costs, such as the foregone revenue from oil not exported because of the war—a particularly dubious claim given that the weak world oil markets during the mid-1980s would almost certainly have prevented Iran from selling much more oil than it did irrespective of the war. In fact, the direct damage from the war was almost entirely confined to border regions with less than 5 percent of the population, a few industrial sites elsewhere that were hit by bombings, and a handful of sites hit by the largely inaccurate missiles. While the war's direct damage to the capital stock was small, a more important effect may have been that the war strained Iran's infrastructure, leaving it in poor condition. The road system became congested as Iran had to ship nearly all imports from Bandar Abbas, the port at the mouth of the Persian Gulf, rather than from the ports further up the Gulf, which are nearer to the country's population centers. The electricity generating plants had to be run continuously at full capacity as Iraq targeted the plants to keep capacity below the level of demand. Oil refineries were run at above capacity to make up for losses to Iraqi attacks and the increased demand created by the Iranian war machine. Years of intense use left these infrastructure facilities threadbare, in a state that would require tens of

---

[1] *MEED Iran Quarterly Report,* June 1992.

billions of dollars during the 1990s for accelerated programs of repair and replacement.

• *Inefficient use of capital, because of priority given to poorly managed state-owned enterprises.* Priority allocation of credits and imports has been given to these enterprises and to white elephant investments. At a time when the world was already awash in cheap steel, revolutionary Iran spent $4.7 billion on the Mobarakeh steel complex near Isfahan which took a decade to build before starting initial production in 1991.[1] Iran plans to spend $1.2 billion on further investments at its three current steel mills, and it is considering another $1.0 billion for a fourth major mill.[2] The Heavy Industry Ministry plans to spend $2.0 billion on twelve state-owned plants including a heavy diesel engine plant, a heavy machine tools plant, and a forging machinery plant—a list which seems more designed for weapons output than for profit, given Iran's dismal record with heavy industry.[3] Similarly, at a time when all the major industrial countries have excess capacity for vehicle manufacture, Iran is putting several billion dollars into car and truck assembly plants, which will require imports nearly equal to the cost of importing completed vehicles. Investments in agro-industry have similarly gone toward the gigantic and dubious, such as the $400 million Mazendaran paper complex and $500 million for seven sugar complexes in Khuzestan.[4]

• *A population growing at about 3 percent per annum.*[5] This requires continuing high investment to provide adequate

---

[1] *MEED*, February 21, 1992.

[2] *MEED*, February 21, 1992. The other two major mills are the 20-year old Soviet mill in Isfahan proper and the war-damaged Ahwaz plant.

[3] *Resalat*, August 17, 1992, as printed in *Akhbaar*, August 18, 1992.

[4] *MEED*, July 3, 1992 and June 5, 1992.

[5] Health and Education Minister Malekzadeh claimed that population growth had been brought down to 2.7 percent (*Ettela'at*, April 12, 1992, as printed in *Akhbaar*, April 12, 1992). The 1986 Census showed population growth of 3.9 percent, but the natural growth (abstracting from the 3.6 million Iraqi and Afghan refugees) was 3.2 percent, according to Majlis Plan and Budget Committee Chairman Alviri in *Keyhan*, November 30,

housing and employment. Job creation will be a particular challenge. Twenty-six million Iranians are under fifteen years of age.[1] Each year 750,000 men turn eighteen, while fewer than 100,000 turn sixty, which suggests Iran needs to create 650,000 more jobs merely to keep the number of unemployed from rising above the 1.7 million who were out of work in 1991-92.[2] Given that total employment in Iran is only 12.9 million, employment has to expand 5 percent each year to absorb the new entrants.

Few means to generate capital

• *Low domestic savings.* Consumers seek to regain the living standard they experienced under the Shah but have seen cut in half since the Revolution. There are signs that when income rises, the increment goes into consumption rather than into the investment needed for future growth. For instance, the explosive growth in imports to $25 billion in 1991-92 was fueled by imports of consumer goods and inputs to manufacture consumer goods.[3] Part of the problem with boosting savings is that the Islamic Republic has had an inefficient banking system. The Central Bank has refused to

---

1989. In fact, the 2.7 percent figure is probably too low; the declining usefulness of ration cards, among other factors, probably led to a more accurate and lower reported population.

[1] Data on population under fifteen and on employment from the Statistical Center of Iran, *Salaam*, March 9, 1992, as cited in *Akhbaar*, March 9, 1992.

[2] Statistical Center of Iran data cited in *Iran Times*, July 10, 1992. Labor force entrance and departure estimated from population data and structure of labor force and population in the *Annual Statistical Yearbook 1990-91*. The employment problem is even greater than stated in the text because unemployment is artificially reduced by policies discouraging women from working unless they are highly educated.

[3] Imports on a customs basis (including shipping) were $28 billion, which translates into $25 billion on a balance-of-payments basis (excluding shipping), Central Bank Governor Aadeli, *Jomhuri Islami*, August 22, 1992.

allow Islamic banking to function effectively.[1] Instead of following the spirit of the Koran's injunction against interest, the Central Bank has enforced rules that make Islamic banking into a sham, with interest existing in all but name. Worse, the Central Bank has forced all banks to pay depositors the same low rate of "profit"—below the rate of inflation, which means individuals keep their funds outside of banks, with the result that the banks lack resources with which to stimulate investment. To complement its policies that depress private savings, the Iranian government, during most years, has not been able to raise sufficient tax revenue to finance its current expenditures, meaning that public savings have been negative.

• *Declining income from oil, as its fields age and its domestic oil consumption increases.* The National Iranian Oil Company was allocated $5.85 billion in 1991-92 primarily to finance its program to raise oil output from 3.5 million barrels per day (mbd) to 4.5 mbd with capacity for surging for short periods to 5.0 mbd. That leaves Iran short of the 6.5 mbd capacity it had before the Revolution.[2] More importantly, the capacity per capita will be 31.5 barrels per year, compared with 68.5 barrels per annum in 1978-79. Another way of expressing the same quandary is that Iran is consuming more and more of its oil output domestically. Consumption in 1991 was 1.1 mbd.[3] The

---

[1] Islamic banking can be fully compatible with economic efficiency. See Zubair Iqbal and Abbas Mirakhar, *Islamic Banking*, International Monetary Fund Occasional Paper No. 49, 1987.

[2] Oil Minister Aqazadeh, *Ronaq*, as printed in *Akhbaar* October 1, 1990 set forth the program; *MEED*, February 21, 1992 reports it is continuing apace.

[3] Oil Minister Aqazadeh, cited in *Iran Focus*, January 1991, said refineries produced 920,000 b/d and imports were 234,000 b/d, at a time when there were essentially no exports of refined products. However, *MEED*, July 3, 1992 reports refinery output at 909,000, imports at 114,000, and exports of refined products at 88,000, for domestic consumption of 935,000.

expansion of output is coming at higher and higher cost; the investment costs could run $3.50 per barrel.[1]

• *Limited prospects for borrowing.* In theory, Iran could borrow abroad in order to grow, and repay the debt. The greater likelihood is that borrowing abroad would create a debt crisis as Iran attempts to meet high capital needs without generating sufficient revenue from domestic savings and oil production. Already in the summer of 1992, Iran had serious trouble paying short-term trade credits. While at first Iran claimed that the problems were caused by a number of payments coming due at the same time, the problem persisted for months, demonstrating that the fundamental issue was over-indebtedness. Iran had exhausted its liquid foreign reserves; holdings in international banks were drawn down by $5.5 billion in 1991-92, to a point that Iran's net position with the banks became negative.[2] In addition to its use of short-term credits (much of which has been arranged by private Iranian businessmen), Iran has secured $15 billion in longer-term loan commitments and used $6-7 billion according to Central Bank.[3] These funds are used disproportionately for state-guaranteed or state-owned projects, many of which will do little to add to Iran's ability to service its debt in the future, leaving the country with an even heavier debt burden and little prospect of being able to service that debt adequately. As its debt situation deteriorates, Iran will find that the attitude of international banks changes from eagerness to lend to an under-borrowed country to wariness about loans to a heavily indebted nation with mediocre payment prospects.

• *Poor conditions for foreign investment.* Rafsanjani has won an internal dispute over whether to woo foreign investors. Iran

---

[1] $10 billion to produce one mbd, amortized over fifteen years at 10 percent interest. However, Oil Minister Aqazadeh claims that the investment needed will be only $3 billion in foreign exchange (*Abrar*, February 4, 1991, as printed in *Akhbaar*, February 4, 1991).

[2] Bank for International Settlements, *International Banking Developments*, various dates, show Iran with net holdings of $5.2 billion in international banks in March 1990 and negative $0.3 billion in December 1991.

[3] Central Bank Governor Aadeli, *Jomhuri Islami*, August 22, 1992.

has revived and liberalized the Shah's foreign investment law in a bid to attract foreign funds, and officials regularly encourage such investments. Some projects are indeed under way, mostly with financing from Dubai businessmen of Iranian background who may be motivated by politics as much as economics. The most advanced project is the al-Mahdi aluminum smelter near Bandar Abbas. The $2 billion smelter complex, which includes an associated power plant, is 60 percent owned by the Iranian government and 40 percent by IDC of Dubai, which is in turn jointly owned by Dubai businessman Mahdi al-Tajir, the British firm George Wimpey, and the Swiss metals trader Marc Rich.[1] In addition, Abdul Wahab Galadari Sons of Dubai has secured permission for a $450 million methyl tertiary butyl ether (MTBE) plant in Bandar Khomeini.[2] At the same time, Iran is not likely to attract large-scale investment by multinational corporations, which are chary because of policy swings in the past, cash-strapped by the world stagnation, and confronted by a host of competing opportunities in the reforming countries of the Eastern bloc and in the newly industrializing nations.

In theory, Iran could adopt an extensive economic reform program that would increase economic efficiency, make better use of Iran's extensive business and technical human capital, and attract financing from abroad, especially from expatriate Iranians. Strong steps towards reform were indeed taken during the first two years of the Rafsanjani government, as described above.

But the reform program stalled in 1991-92, largely because it was undermining the privileged position of clerics and their allies. As one Iranian businessman told the *Wall Street Journal*, "Mullah capitalism is thriving on the remains of once-profitable businesses" which the government has handed over to "foundations" that are "cornucopias of privilege for well-connected clerics."[3] Data about the foundations is scarce, but

---

[1] *Financial Times*, March 26, 1992. Marc Rich was formerly a U.S. citizen.

[2] *MEED*, February 21, 1992.

[3] Peter Waldman, "Mullahs Keep Control of Iranian Economy with an Iron Hand," *Wall Street Journal*, May 5, 1992.

Rafsanjani estimated in 1989 that the foundations and the government controlled 70-80 percent of Iran's factories between them.[1] Scandals have shaken some of the smaller foundations, usually controlled by minor clerics and their friends. One particularly juicy episode saw Majlis Member Ghaffuri lamely contesting documentary evidence that his Al-Hadi Foundation had imported skimpy women's underwear at the official exchange rate for sale at a large markup.[2] Rafsanjani has had to move slowly against the larger foundations, by publicizing corruption and slowly securing resignations of their leaders. The optimistic view would be that he will be able to resume the reform program after assuming control over the foundations; the pessimistic view is that reforms will be at too slow a pace to save Iran from a debt-cum-poverty crisis.

Perhaps the two most positive indicators of the state of the reform program would be the adoption of a realistic exchange rate and allowing Iranian expatriates to come and go freely. Both points are key to restoring economic growth; both saw considerable progress in 1989-90; both have been the object of sustained campaigns by radicals; and both saw mixed signals in 1991-92.

Rafsanjani, at the start of his presidency, liberalized the much-feared exit controls at Tehran airport to permit nearly all visiting expatriates to leave freely. The finance minister and Central Bank governor then met in 1991 with several hundred expatriates in New York to urge them to return.[3] But the outraged radicals struck back with a vigorous campaign that resulted in the tightening of exit controls, though some expatriates continue to return.[4]

---

[1] *Jomhuri Islami*, December 10, 1989, as printed in *Akhbaar*, December 10, 1989.

[2] *Iran Times*, August 24, 1990. Other scandals have involved the Raja and Alba Foundations; cf. *Resalat*, May 10, 1990, as printed in *Akhbaar*, May 10, 1990.

[3] *Abrar*, May 4, 1991, as printed in *Akhbaar*, May 4, 1991.

[4] See Elaine Sciolino, "Iran Struggles to Attract Investors from Abroad," *New York Times*, April 30, 1992, *Economist*, May 2, 1992, and Caryle

On the exchange rate, the Rafsanjani government has rejected a policy of formal devaluations for the old official rate of about seventy rials per dollar; instead, it has progressively shifted transactions from that rate to the freely floating rate, now about 1,450 rials per dollar, or to intermediate rates. In 1989-90, exchange rate dealers were legalized, and more realistic exchange rates for consumer good imports were introduced.[1] Exporters were allowed a more favorable exchange rate; as a result, non-oil exports rose from $1.0 billion in 1988-89 to $2.6 billion in 1991-92.

However, there was little movement on the exchange rate front between the reforms of January 1991[2] and the end of 1992, despite frequent announcements that there would be only one exchange rate by March 1993. The official exchange rate was still used to make imports of some basic foodstuffs artificially cheap, as well as to enrich those able to import at the official rate and then sell at prices that reflect the free rate (as in the Al-Hadi Foundation case cited above). Corruption was inevitable in a situation of pervasive double prices—butchers, for example, simultaneously sold subsidized beef to those with ration coupons for 750 rials per kilogram while selling the rest of their beef at 3,000 rials per kilo.[3] The average exchange rate for industrial inputs moved little from 1990 through 1992, from about 200 to about 300 (on a weighted average basis). In December 1992, Rafsanjani proposed moving all transactions except a few priority goods (such as basic foodstuffs) to the floating rate effective in March 1993, but opposition in the Majlis to such a step has been strong.

The difficulties Rafsanjani has had in implementing reforms suggests that Iran may not be able to sustain its recent growth burst. Vested interests may fight to preserve economic

---

Murphy, "Iran Poised for Resurgence of Business," *Washington Post*, April 18, 1992.

[1] See *Keyhan*, October 13, 1989, as printed in *Akhbaar*, October 13, 1989, and *Keyhan*, September 23, 1990, as printed in *Akhbaar*, September 23, 1990.

[2] Those reforms are described in *MEED*, February 1, 1991.

[3] *Iran Times*, June 2, 1989 and personal observation in Tehran, November 1989.

inefficiencies from which they gain, like unprofitable state enterprises and the complex exchange rate system that diverts energy from productive activity into speculation. The most likely medium-term path for the Iranian economy seems to be to continue slow reforms, even in the face of considerable opposition, to produce growth at a rate well below that necessary to satisfy popular expectations.

Since Iran's rulers have staked their credibility on delivering prosperity, but may not be able to do so by the mid or late 1990s, Iran may well become desperate to find alternatives. Ambitious development projects (many of them ill-conceived) could be stalled half-built, while external funds dry up as Iran is unable to service its debt. In short, Iran could be desperate for additional resources. Under these circumstances, there might well be some in Tehran who would propose a redistribution of resources from the oil-rich states on the other side of the Persian Gulf.

In other words, the push for prosperity by the moderates is not necessarily a stabilizing influence. Indeed, Tehran's focus on economic growth rather than Islamic purity as the main activity of the government could become a new source of instability in the region, if Iranians conclude that the shortest and least painful route to prosperity lies in pressuring their neighbors. That pressure could take various forms, some of them relatively benign—e.g., a hard sell for Gulf investment in Iranian projects along the lines of the proposed aluminum complex in Bandar Abbas. Surely some in Tehran would consider using the newly rebuilt Iranian military as a means of pressure. It is difficult to imagine Iran mounting a Saddam-style takeover of Bahrain, Qatar, or the UAE, but the Islamic Republic has shown great ingenuity in using its military to achieve its aims in unexpected ways (from crossing marshes in Iraq to mining the Gulf).

REASSERTION OF PERSIAN NATIONALISM

The fact that Iran's moderates place a higher priority on economic prosperity than do the radicals is one reason to worry that the moderates may pursue a more aggressive policy in the Gulf than would the radicals. Another is that the moderates are more susceptible to the call of Persian nationalism.[1] Khomeini objected to displays of Persian nationalism as glorifying Iran's pre-Islamic past and as incompatible with the unity of believers. He insisted that the Majlis be renamed the Islamic Majlis, not the National Majlis. Some of his more enthusiastic followers wished to bulldoze the ancient city of Persepolis, but they were restrained. Still, Persian nationalism is a suspect concept for radicals, for whom the natural sphere of action is the Islamic world.

The principal arena in which Persian nationalist impulses have been expressed in modern times has been the Gulf. Many Iranians deeply believe in the Persian character of the Persian Gulf. They see Iran as the inheritor of a great civilization, whereas, just a generation ago, the Gulf Arabs were barefoot lizard-eaters, as they are described in a Persian insult. After all, God chose the Arabs to conquer the world in the name of Islam so that the world would realize that this conquest was due to God alone. In other words, God chose the Arabs since the world believed them incapable of such conquests, and thus ascribed the ascendancy of Islam to God alone.

More prosaically, Iran has, for several decades, felt that it has a natural role as protector of the Gulf. Iran has never ruled the southern (Arab) side of the Gulf, and Iranian politics have long been oriented more to the country's central plateau and north rather than to the seacoast. But that was partly because the Gulf was such an underdeveloped and sparsely populated area. Important Iranian communities have developed in most of the smaller Gulf countries; indeed, the choice of 1925 as the cutoff arrival date for what distinguishes a first-class (voting) from a second-class (non-voting) Kuwaiti citizen was designed to disenfranchise the descendants of Iranian immigrants. The Iranian government maintains hospitals, schools, and other social institutions in a number of locations on the Arab side of the Gulf, services which may have been necessary when that

---

[1] For a brief history of Iran and an account of how that history is perceived by ordinary Iranians, see John Limbert, *Iran: At War with History* (Boulder: Westview Press, 1987), pp. 46-62. The classic work on Persian nationalism is Richard Cotton, *Nationalism in Iran* (Pittsburgh: University of Pittsburgh Press, 1979). Cotton emphasizes fissiparous tendencies in Iran, but he also notes the superior attitudes towards the Gulf Arabs, pp. 338-339.

area was poverty-stricken but which are now primarily an exercise in Iranian power-projection.

By the time the British decided in the late 1960s to withdraw from the Gulf, Iran was determined to dominate the area. In part, Iran was concerned about radical unrest, which was building in Oman and had some support in Bahrain. In addition, the Shah had territorial ambitions, and first mentioned an Iranian claim to Bahrain shortly before 1971, when that country, Oman, the UAE, and Qatar were given independence from Britain. At the same time, Iran landed troops on Abu Musa and two other small islands near the mouth of the Gulf which had been administered by the British as part of the predecessor of the UAE. An agreement was signed allowing Iran to maintain troops on the half of Abu Musa it seized while allowing continued administration of the populated area by their previous ruler, the sheikh of Sharjah, as part of the newly independent United Arab Emirates; simultaneously, Iran gave up its claim on Bahrain.

Shortly after the 1979 Revolution, Tehran fomented pro-Iranian movements in the Gulf, most notoriously the Iranian-sponsored attempt to overthrow the Bahraini government in December 1981. Thereafter, radical governments confined themselves to periodic outbursts of rhetoric, e.g., demanding that the Gulf be referred to as the Persian Gulf. The moderate Rafsanjani government has taken a more domineering attitude towards the Gulf than did the earlier radical governments.

The most obvious example is the renewed pressure on the UAE over Abu Musa. In March 1992, Rafsanjani visited the island. Within a month, Iran violated the 1971 agreement by expelling several hundred residents, including all those who were not UAE nationals, and took over the electrical and water utilities. On August 24, Iran stepped up the pressure by turning back a ferry carrying 104 passengers, mostly Egyptian teachers and their families but also the island's governor Bashir Ahmad Ibrahim.[1] U.S. officials have speculated that Iran may be preparing to build a naval base on the island,

---

[1] *Mideast Mirror*, September 4, 1992. See also *Abrar*, August 26, 1992, *Reuters*, April 15, 1992, and *New York Times*, April 16, 1992.

which lies in the middle of the shipping lanes used by oil tankers.[1]

In response to strong criticism from the Arab states of the Gulf, Iran dug in its heels. Although Foreign Minister Velayati traced the crisis to what he described as junior Iranian officials, Iran refused to return to the *status quo ante*.[2] Talks over the islands broke down in late September 1992, and the GCC states brought the issue to the UN.[3] When the GCC states at their December 1992 meeting restated their criticism of Iran's violations of "historical precedents," the Iranian press escalated the affair by reviving Iran's claims to sovereignty over Bahrain.

> If 'historical precedents' are to be the criteria, the Shaykh of Bahrain should go about his own business and the sovereignty of the people of Iran over the land of Bahrain, which belonged to Iran until 1972, should be reestablished. *It would be appropriate for the Iranian foreign minister to seriously propose the issue of the Islamic Republic of Iran's sovereignty over Bahrain* on the basis of indisputable 'historical precedents' with which all the regional shaykhs are well acquainted, and *should launch an earnest and effective effort to terminate Bahrain's separation from Iran.* (emphasis added)[4]

Other episodes of moderate-led Iranian muscle-flexing in the Gulf have taken the form of financial pressure on Kuwait and Qatar. Iraq had flown six passenger planes belonging to Kuwait Airways to Iran during the Gulf War. Iran insisted for more than a year that it would return the planes, but took no action to do so. Finally, the Iranians presented a bill for $95 million in "parking fees," later reducing the sum to a mere

---

[1] Chris Hedges, "Iran is Riling Its Gulf Neighbors, Pressing Claim to Three Disputed Isles," *New York Times*, September 13, 1992.

[2] Nora Boustany, "Iran Seeks Wider Mideast Role," *Washington Post*, October 12, 1992.

[3] Youssef Ibrahim, "Dispute over Gulf Islands Worsens Iran-Arab Ties," *New York Times*, October 4, 1992.

[4] *Jomhuri Islami* editorial December 27, 1992, as printed in *FBIS-NES-93-004*, January 7, 1993, pp. 42-43.

$87.5 million. The "fees" were such a transparent ransom demand that Iran became embarrassed; it returned the planes in August and September 1992 though continued to press its claim for payment.[1] Iran successfully pressured Kuwait into paying $10 million as compensation for losses by Iranian workers.[2]

Iran has been playing hardball with Qatar over the world's largest gas field, which lies primarily under Qatari waters but partly extends into Iranian waters. Iran has signed a $2 billion contract for development of its section by an Italian-Russian consortium.[3] Iran plans to produce 1.2 billion cubic feet per day of gas and 50,000 barrels per day (b/d) of oil by 1995 from what it calls the South Pars field. The potential for abuse in draining a common resource is obvious, especially since Iran seems eager to begin exploiting the field before Qatar can do so. It hardly seems accidental that the Qatari authorities have recently acceded to Iranian suggestions that they let a multi-million contract to design a pipeline to provide water to Qatar from Iran's Karun River. The pipeline may indeed be the least expensive means to provision Qatar, but it is hard to believe that the Qatari rulers would sleep better at night knowing that control of their water tap is in Iranian hands.

The Iranians feel their northern and eastern borders are as artificially confining as their southern. After all, the great epic poem that defines Iranian nationalism, the *Shahnameh*, is set mostly in Afghanistan and the newly-independent republics of Central Asia, which was also home to Zoroaster, the towering giant of pre-modern Persian culture. Ayatollah Taheri, the religious leader of Isfahan, recently asserted,

---

[1] *New York Times*, April 16, 1992; *Iran Times*, June 26, 1992 and July 24, 1992; VIRI, July 27, 1992, as printed in *FBIS-NES*-92-146, July 29, 1992, p. 47.

[2] *MEED*, March 1, 1991. Iran reported 50,000 of its nationals fled Kuwait to Iran after August 2, 1990 (*Iran Times*, September 14, 1990), not counting the larger group of second class (non-voting) Kuwaitis of Iranian heritage.

[3] *MEED*, March 6, 1992 and February 21, 1992.

> Now some of the newly-independent republics of the former
> Soviet Union do not agree to the ignominious Turkmanchai
> Treaty between Iran and the former Soviet Union [actually
> Russia] and consider themselves part of Iran and regard the
> esteemed leader [Khamenei] as their own leader.[1]

A more mainstream Iranian viewpoint would be that Iran will
naturally have a major influence in the region. Moderate
Iranians are more prone to these temptations than are radicals,
for whom the key issue is Islam, not geopolitical influence.

A good example of their conflicting agendas is the
maneuvering in Afghanistan. Iranian radicals were long
lukewarm in their support for the Afghan mujahedeen
because they were Sunni and some were primarily
nationalists. Under the Rafsanjani government, Iran has been
cooperating with Persian-speaking forces that are uninterested
in a religious government rather than with those like
Hekmatayar who base their program on religion dominating
public life.[2] Iranian moderates are the ones who have moved to
support Persian-speakers in the new government, such as
Defense Minister Ahmad Shah Masood and Commander-in-
Chief General Asif Dilawar.

It is difficult to judge whether Iranian expansive pressure
may be directed to the north or to the south, though the wealth
of its southern neighbors must be an extra temptation.
However, the Western response in the two cases would be
different. The issue of Iran's role in Central Asia and
Afghanistan, important as it may be for those in the area, is not
of key importance to the West, simply because the states
concerned are not vital to U.S. interests.

A COUNTERTREND: UNPOPULARITY AT HOME MAY LIMIT ACTION ABROAD

One factor that does make the moderates less dangerous to
the West than the radicals is that moderates are showing
themselves to be technocratic elites isolated from the common
folk and from the social mores of society. The Rafsanjani

---

[1] *Kar va Kargar,* as printed in *Akhbaar,* February 26, 1992.

[2] *Iran Times,* September 18, 1992.

government relies heavily on Western-educated and Western-oriented elites in the professions and in business circles. While this social group is important for the functioning of Iran as a modern society, its numbers are not large, and its members live, think, and function in ways quite distinct from that of most Iranians. They are not oriented towards building coalitions or towards mobilizing popular support; they think they know what needs to be done, and they want to do it.

As for the common folk, the moderates have demonstrated a striking ability to alienate all and please none. The business community regards the moderates as too timid at tackling the tangle of red tape and corruption and as not competent enough to deliver real growth. The popular attitude is partly indifference, as evidenced by the low voter turnout for the spring 1992 Majlis elections. But the technocrats have taken a series of actions that have infuriated the poor, most notably a campaign to dispossess those without clear land title, some of whom are simple squatters but most of whom possess a disputed title to the land. Riots by squatters broke out in several cities in spring 1992.

The riots in Mashad on May 30, 1992 may have been more than a violent expression of discontent by squatters, of the sort that shook several other Iranian cities that spring. The Mashad riots appear to have been well organized; the Association for the Protection of the Rights of the Low-Earners in Society distributed leaflets claiming responsibility. As many as forty people may have died in the rioting. The targets appear to have been well planned; damage was confined to government buildings and adjacent shops.[1]

Other signs of discontent abound. Labor and Social Affairs Minister Hossain Kamali spoke of 2,000 strikes from March through September 1991.[2] Workers at the Isfahan steel mill went on a sit-down strike in September 1992.[3] *Jomhuri Islami* reported several deaths in a bombing on August 29 at Behesht-e

---

[1]   *Economist,* June 13, 1992.

[2]   *MEED,* February 21, 1992.

[3]   *Keyhan,* September 18, 1992.

Zahara cemetery.[1] An arson attack in the Tehran bazaar on September 22 caused an estimated $1 million in damage.[2]

One reason that discontent has resulted in violent protests is that the moderates have systematically reduced other channels for its expression. As explained above, Rafsanjani manipulated election procedures in 1992 to exclude most of his opponents from the Majlis. He has reduced the role of the Majlis; for instance, he refused to allow the Majlis to exercise its responsibilities, such as the confirmation of ministers. The Majlis had been the outlet for discontent and the source of the regime's information about which of its policies lacked public support. Meanwhile, the newspapers have become less free-wheeling in their criticism of the government. An example is the government-organized coverage of the Mashad riots; the events were ignored for several days until an official line was developed. Pre-Rafsanjani public disturbances (such as university unrest over dorms or exams) were reported promptly and disagreement over the authorities' response was common.

The suppression of criticism and the undermining of democracy in Iran may conflict with the image that the word "moderate" brings to mind in the West. In fact, Rafsanjani's group has promoted personal and property rights through a stable system of law administered by neutral judges. The sort of despotism experienced under the radicals at their worst—punishments inflicted without rhyme or reason on the whim of whatever judge (in many cases self-appointed) heard the case—is less in evidence.

But the reduced channels for expression of discontent carries a severe risk. As Jean Gueyras wrote in *Le Monde,*

> The elimination of the radicals from Parliament is a double-edged sword. The Third Majlis, which in the end did not seriously limit Rafsanjani's plans, offered an escape valve for popular discontent. The risk is that the discontent will from now on be expressed in public places. Furthermore, the current power-

---

[1] *Le Monde,* September 1, 1992.

[2] *New York Times,* September 23, 1992.

holders can no longer blame the opposition for the eventual failure of their plans.[1]

Much of the Iranian public has been alienated from the government for some years. However, the radicals were able to command strong support from a minority group of revolutionary devotees. The moderates command indifferent support at best from these hard-core revolutionaries. Rafsanjani has alienated many of them with his campaign to gut the revolutionary institutions, which continue to command respect from a non-negligible proportion of the population. The "followers of Khomeini's line," as the hard-core revolutionaries like to call themselves, are not going to turn out in the same numbers and with the same enthusiasm for the moderates as they did for the earlier more radial governments. For example, in Mashad, the second-most holy, clerical city in Iran, there was no popular militia that came together spontaneously to defend the Revolution. The suppression of the riots instead required the intervention of the police and militia.

The high level of public alienation, the lack of channels in which to express discontent, the fading support from the regime's natural base of support, the domination of technocrats without political sense—all of these trends make the Rafsanjani government look more and more like the Shah's regime from 1971 to 1978. As under the Shah, there is no obvious opposition around which the discontented could rally. And so it is possible that the Islamic Republic is a regime which continues because there is no alternative, not because it commands support. It is stable, but only because of the lack of options.[2] As the Shah discovered in 1978, this kind of stability can erode quickly.

---

[1] *Le Monde*, April 26-27, 1992.

[2] The People's Mojahedeen were a credible alternative in the early 1980s, but they lost popular support when they became de facto allies of Baghdad in the Iraq-Iran War and when their leader, Masood Rajavi, demanded unthinking support despite his peculiar personal behavior (i.e. an embarrassingly quickly-arranged marriage to a woman who had been the wife of a close associate was trumpeted as a great step for women's liberation).

This does not mean that a new revolution is around the corner. Those who participated in the Revolution are unlikely ever to move to overthrow it, because the events of 1978-79 retain a mythic aura. Also, many Iranians are too cynical to risk themselves for any new cause. The profound exhaustion with politics leads to an attitude of ignoring the government and retreat into private life common to authoritarian societies. But, as the new generation that was too young to remember the Shah or fight in the war with Iraq reaches the age of twenty, it could well be moved onto the streets by some crisis. A popular revolution in the 1990s seems improbable, but it would not be surprising if a combination of popular unrest and disgust with the current system led to an abandonment of the Islamic Republic form of government, either through a coup or, more likely, through creeping secularization. The Islamic Revolution has not made the successful transition to a second generation. Hatred for the Shah has faded, as have the hopes for a just society based on the principles of Islam.

In the event that the Islamic Republic fails, the form that a new government would take is hard to predict. Precisely because the current regime is kept in power partly by a lack of alternatives, another option would likely emerge only at the last minute. The situation could well become fluid. One possible source for a new government is the army which has an independence from the current regime because the regime clearly prefers the Revolutionary Guards and *komitehs*. Moreover, the army has some experienced and competent leaders and is not, like many government institutions, tainted by corruption or rife with top officials whose only qualification is their good political connections.

One common way to analyze Islamic Iran is to ask whether the Revolution has moderated, on the theory that if pragmatism prevails, then the U.S. can find a *modus vivendi* with Iran, although the two states may still differ on many points. The aim of the analysis here is to reject that viewpoint.

Iran's moderates do not differ profoundly from its radicals with respect to foreign policy, in contrast to the bitter disputes between them over domestic economic and social affairs. Furthermore, to the extent that the two groups do disagree on foreign policy issues, the moderates pose a greater threat to the West than the radicals. The moderates add an aspect of Persian nationalism to the anti-Western vision of Islam which they share with the radicals. This combination, in concrete terms, has meant that the moderates hold ambitious aspirations to dominate the Persian Gulf and to play a major role in the Levant, the Caucasus and Central Asia, if not further afield. On a positive note, they have slightly tempered the radical conception that the Islamic Republic is a defender of ideology offensive to the Western concept of human rights, but, by basing their claim to legitimacy in part upon promises of economic prosperity that may be unfulfillable, the moderates have added a new element of danger—they may be tempted to seize what they cannot produce themselves from their oil-rich neighbors in order to fulfill these promises of economic prosperity. Yet perhaps the most important way the moderates may present a more dangerous challenge to the West is their attempt to build Iran's professional military into a regional superpower.

II SIGNALING INTENTIONS? THE MILITARY BUILD-UP

A further worrying aspect of the ascendancy of the moderates is that they are acquiring the means to be a greater military threat than was radical-dominated Iran. The radicals never trusted the military enough to provide it with ample resources, nor did they see the military as vital to their plans to expand Iran's influence abroad. The moderates, on the other hand, have more respect for the military and for the uses to which it may be put.

During the years in which Iranian moderates and radicals contested for power, Iranian military might declined, a decline greatly exacerbated by the war with Iraq and the inability of the radical governments to mobilize support for that war. Because the radicals were unwilling to recognize the reality that Iraq could not be conquered, their insistence on "war until victory" bled Iran for little purpose. While the war ground up Iran's pre-revolutionary store of advanced weaponry, the radicals were unable to generate public support for a serious arms acquisition program or for a large domestic military machine. Iranian military spending actually fell during the war, though it could be argued that the numbers are distorted by the unwillingness of suppliers to sell to Iran and by Iran's artificial exchange rate.[1]

---

[1] The military budget went from 375 billion rials in 1980-81 to 526 billion rials in 1988-89. In constant 1974-5 prices (using the GDP deflator), the military budget was 141 billion rials in 1980-1 and 67

Perhaps a better way to measure the war effort is to look at the size of the military relative to the population. Iran used a manpower-intensive strategy, so its military should have been expected to be large relative to the population. However, the military, in its broadest sense (including the Baseej and Guard units), was rarely more than sixteen per thousand population, compared with eleven in pre-revolutionary Iran, sixty in Jordan, forty-four in Israel, twenty-eight in Cuba, twenty in Singapore and Greece.[1] Rather than a *levee en masse*, revolutionary Iran had a minor military for its size.

One important reason for the armed forces' relatively small size was that the radical governments distrusted the regular military. The radical priority was creating ideologically pure institutions, starting with the Revolutionary Guards and later the Baseej militia. The radicals were not keen on maintaining or modernizing Iran's existing high technology weapon systems, as those systems came from the United States. Radical governments preferred to acquire new weapon systems from Third World sources like North Korea, although they were often of a less advanced design. The new weapon systems were frequently assigned to the Guards, who were less skilled at integrating advanced technology with their infantry forces. Sometimes the combination of dedicated Guards and simple new technologies worked, as in the assault through the marshes on Majnoon Island, however, often it did not.

ARMS PURCHASES FROM EASTERN BLOC COUNTRIES

The moderates under Rafsanjani have gone far towards reversing the radicals' policy and turning the military into a more powerful force. CIA Director Robert Gates reported in June 1992 that Iran has embarked on an "across-the-board effort" to develop it military and defense industries, including

---

billion rials in 1988-89. The budget included the vast majority of war costs, but not all of them.

[1] Data for countries besides Iran from U.S. Arms Control and Disarmament Agency [ACDA], *World Military Expenditures and Arms Transfers 1990*, p. 41. ACDA shows the Iranian military ratio peaking at 12.6 per thousand in 1988.

weapons of mass destruction.[1] The policy of rearmament was Rafsanjani's brain child. Shortly after assuming the presidency in July 1989, Rafsanjani visited Moscow and signed the Islamic Republic's first agreement for major weapon systems, including a reported forty-eight MiG-29 fighters and one hundred T-72 tanks in a deal said to be worth a total of $1.9 billion.[2] The Five Year Plan, prepared by Rafsanjani and approved in January 1990, included a provision for $10 billion in foreign exchange for weapons, as well as $2 billion in 1990-94 for the Defense Industrial Organization.[3]

Since then, reports of weapons purchases have steadily mounted. Jack Nelson of the *Los Angeles Times* described an Iranian arms buildup that is "fast making it the dominant military power in the Middle East," thanks to extraordinarily low prices for Soviet arms, perhaps even as low as $50,000 per T-72 tank.[4] Kenneth Timmerman reported that, during a visit to Moscow in July 1991, the head of the Iranian Air Force, General Mansur Sattari, and his Soviet counterpart, Lieutenant General [and later CIS Defense Minister] Yevgeny Shaposhnikov, signed a $6 billion deal. Russian officials involved in the negotiations said in interviews at the Dubai Air Show that it covered the delivery of one hundred MiG-29 fighters, forty-eight MiG-31 high altitude interceptors, a squadron of Sukhoi-24 long-range strike aircraft, two Ilyushin IL-76 aircraft equipped as airborne early warning planes, and

---

[1] R. Jeffrey Smith, *Washington Post*, June 16, 1992.

[2] Kenneth Timmerman, *Weapons of Mass Destruction: The Cases of Iran, Syria, and Libya* (Los Angeles: Simon Wiesenthal Center, August 1992), p. 13.

[3] *Keyhan*, April 18, 1990 as printed in *Akhbaar*, April 18, 1990. Iran's military industry was handed a significant blow when the Iran Helicopter Industries main center in Tehran was destroyed in a suspicious September 1992 blaze; it had produced parts that allowed much of Iran's 300-helicopter fleet to stay in the air (*Iran Times*, September 18, 1992).

[4] *Los Angeles Times*, January 7, 1992. Nelson described the price as rumored; the rumors seem unlikely to be accurate.

the construction of a MiG-29 assembly plant in Iran.[1] Jacques Issard wrote in *Le Monde* that Iran had spent $2 billion for forty-eight MiG-29s (having received twenty in 1991), twenty-four MiG-31s, twenty-four MiG-27 close support aircraft, twelve older Tupolev-222M heavy bombers, and two Ilyushin IL-76.[2] Youssef Ibrahim wrote in the *New York Times* that Iranian arms agreements had totaled $7 billion.[3]

Iran has approached other ex-Soviet republics and East European states. During his visit to Tehran in April 1992, Ukrainian President Leonid Kravchuk signed an agreement to purchase twenty-nine million barrels of Iranian oil (four million tons) in return for Ukrainian machine parts, building materials, and—according to some reports—arms.[4] In March 1991, Czechoslovakia signed a $1.5 billion deal with Iran to import oil, and Iran requested to be paid in heavy machinery and arms.[5]

Iran has also negotiated arms deals with China and North Korea. It has signed a contract for a new fleet of seventy-ton Chinese patrol boats equipped with Styx anti-ship missiles, F-7 fighters, surface-to-air missiles, and artillery.[6] According to *Le Monde,* Iran has, with North Korean aid, built facilities to produce both SCUD-Cs with a range of 500-km and No-Dong-1s with a range of 1,000-km (disturbingly close to being within

---

[1] Timmerman, *Weapons of Mass Destruction,* p. 13.

[2] Jacques Issard, "Le Rearmement de l'Iran Preocupe les Occidentaux," *Le Monde,* July 25, 1992.

[3] Youssef Ibrahim, *New York Times,* August 8, 1992.

[4] *Financial Times,* April 30, 1992. In January, the Ukrainian Deputy Prime Minister stated that the barter deal, for which a first agreement was signed, could include the sale of weapons (*Financial Times,* January 30, 1992).

[5] *MEED* and *Financial Times,* March 22, 1991.

[6] Rowan Scarborough, "China to Boost Iran's Navy," *Washington Times,* April 22, 1992.

range of Israel, which is only 1,100 km from Iran).[1] The
Defense and Logistics Ministry announced "mass production"
of long-range surface-to-surface missiles in February 1991.[2]
Kenneth Timmerman has reported that Iran first test-fired the
SCUD-C, an improved version of the SCUD-B Iran used during
the war with Iraq, in May 1991 and that Iran subsequently
ordered 170 from North Korea. Nevertheless, he doubts that
Iran could produce the missile without constant help from
North Korean technicians.[3] The London *Sunday Telegraph*
reported that four Syrian army officers were killed in Iran
while working to extend the range of SCUD missiles.[4] Iran
appears to have drawn a lesson from the Gulf War: "Missiles
appear more cost-effective than aircraft, especially as they are
more or less assured of penetration, [and they] will become
more accurate and cheaper and obviate the need to depend on
foreign sources for spare parts, training of pilots and cyclical
replacement."[5]

ASSESSING IRAN'S ARMS PURCHASES

What is the significance of the reports of arms purchases?
There are five reasons to think that these and other reports are
not necessarily a cause for concern:
  • *Iran's purchases have not yet been delivered.* There is an
enormous difference between weapons deliveries and an
agreement to negotiate about arms sales. The agreement to
negotiate has to be followed by a firm contract for a weapons
system, which is then likely to be delivered over a period of

---

[1] Jacques Issard, "Le Rearmement," *Le Monde,* July 25, 1992.

[2] *MEED,* February 8, 1991.

[3] Timmerman, *Weapons of Mass Destruction,* pp. 22-24.

[4] John Bulloch, *Sunday Telegraph,* May 31, 1992.

[5] Shahram Chubin, "Iran and the Lessons of the Gulf War 1991"
(Unpublished manuscript on file with author). See Chubin, "Iran and
Regional Security in the Persian Gulf," *Survival,* Autumn 1992, and
Keyhan International, March 17, 1991, "A Military Lesson from the Persian
Gulf War," as printed in *FBIS-NES-*91-052, March 18, 1991, p. 81.

some years. The published reports about multi-billion-dollar arms agreements are therefore consistent with expenditures which remain within the Majlis-allocated limits. That limit for 1992-93 is $1.2 billion, down from the $1.5 billion the government proposed to the Majlis.[1]

- *The magnitude of the arms purchases acquisition seems to be quite well known.* Although there is no evidence that spending has exceeded the budgeted amounts, the budget contains several discretionary accounts from which several hundred million dollars is probably being spent on secret projects. Islamic Iran has been remarkably open about its defense budget (much more so than was imperial Iran). Allegations that Iran has counter-trade (barter) arrangements with the states of the former Soviet Union for arms deliveries are implausible, given that Iran has been fighting for months with these states over their inability to deliver sufficient goods to Iran to pay for their supply of gas from Iran. Russia has sent special missions to Iran to promise to repay its $600 million debt to Iran in order to prevent Iran from stopping its supply of gas. There are credible reports that the gas flow has stopped at various times because of unpaid bills.

- *Integrating the new weapons into an effective fighting force will take time.* While the commander of the Iranian Air Force, Brigadier General Mansur Sattari, said in February 1992 that Iran has deployed MiG-29s, Sukhoi-24s, and F-7s,[2] it is unlikely that Iran is yet capable of making full use of these weapons' capabilities. The three Kilo-class submarines ordered from Russia in 1989 at a cost of $300 million per sub illustrate some of the problems Iran faces in integrating new systems into their existing military: the construction took several years, the delivery of the first sub was delayed until November 1992 because of the need to train crews at an old Soviet sub base in Estonia, and there was a dispute over the payment schedule. Rear Admiral Edward Sheafer, Jr., U.S. Chief of Naval Intelligence, said "Tehran's ambitions aside, it probably will

---

[1] *Resalat*, April 15, 1992, as printed in *Akhbaar*, April 15, 1992; see also *MEED*, August 28, 1992.

[2] IRNA, February 5, 1992, as printed in *FBIS-NES*-92-025, February 6, 1992, p. 28.

be a long time before the Iranian navy has more than a marginal capability to operate the submarines effectively."[1]

• *The new Soviet equipment will take time before they can be fully operational.* Iran will not, for the next three to five years, be able to rely on its new Soviet-ordered equipment as the backbone of its forces, because of the inevitable delays before deliveries and because training must be completed. During this interval, Iran expects to rely primarily on weapon systems obtained from the West. Defense and Armed Forces Logistics Minister Akbar Torkan set forth the principles of Iran's Five Year Defense Plan in a speech to the Islamic Association of Engineers in April 1992:

> The general policy of this plan is reconstruction and modernization of the existing equipment and weapons because their value in the defense sector is $60 billion at international prices while our five-year defense budget is $9.45 billion of which $450 million belongs to the Disciplinary Force... To modernize what we have is economical... The F-5 is the best airframe and it is going to stay in the world armies for a long time to come. No army in the world except the Iranian Army and the U.S. Navy possess F-14. There are seventy of them. We have more than one hundred warships. The number of our Western and Eastern tanks was above 3,000... This is no small capital... They should be repaired and maintained.[2]

• *Iran will not pose a major threat to its neighbors during the next three to five years because of its reliance on aging Western weapons platforms* and the strength of both Iraq's forces and Saudi Arabia's air force. Iraq still has a much more significant force than Iran can field. Tehran cannot credibly threaten to intervene on behalf of Iraqi Shi'ites, because its military is no match for Baghdad's forces. Since Tehran lacks the equipment to mount a seaborne invasion, and since its air force is no match for the world-class Saudi Air Force, Tehran will not, by itself, pose much of a military threat in the short term to its neighbors on the southern side of the Gulf.

---

[1] Rowan Scarborough, *Washington Times*, April 22, 1992.

[2] Jam Number 4, as printed in *Akhbaar*, June 9, 1992.

Reasons For Concern

In spite of all this, there are several important reasons why the West should be seriously concerned about the implications of the buildup. The military situation in the Gulf is likely to change in Iran's favor by the mid- or late-1990s. Iran is the rising power in the Gulf, while Iraq has declined because of the Gulf War and the UN-imposed sanctions. The short-term threat to Gulf stability comes from Iraq, however Iran will pose the greater threat within a decade.

• *If present trends continue, Iran will have acquired significant numbers of weapons from the Eastern bloc* and will have integrated those weapon systems into a serious fighting force within a decade.

• *An alliance with one or more states in the region could magnify Iran's military power* and thus enable Iran to pose a far greater threat to the West. Several possible scenarios for this to come into being are described below. Although none of the scenarios are very likely in and of themselves, there is a reasonable chance that one could turn into a reality.

• *The threat to Iran from Iraq will diminish over time.* It is therefore not credible to view Iran's weapons program as a response to a continued Iraqi threat. That threat is real in the short term, but within that time frame, Iran cannot acquire and absorb into its active forces the Soviet-bloc equipment that would enable it to block Iraqi aggression. Iran's short-term guarantee of security from Iraqi attack is, ironically, the reaction of the U.S. to renewed Iraqi aggression, for the U.S. and its allies would certainly not permit Iraqi attacks on any of its neighbors. If the Iranian weapons acquisition program is ineffective for short-term defense, it is unnecessary for medium-term defense, because by the time Iran has absorbed the weapons it is buying, Iraq is unlikely to pose much of a military threat. If Saddam or a Saddam-clone remains in power, Iraq will lack the resources to buy many new arms— arms suppliers are likely to maintain considerable restraints even if the sanctions are relaxed and/or the UN eases up on its monitoring of Iraqi high-tech weapons plants. Iraq will find it increasingly difficult to maintain and repair weapons in its aging arsenal because of a lack of cash and barriers to spare parts. On the other hand, if a new kind of government comes to power in Iraq, it is unlikely to devote large resources to the military, given the country's urgent reconstruction needs. So in that case as well, Iraqi military might will deteriorate from its current level.

• *The Iranian military build-up seems designed to provide a "sea denial" capability.* The Kilo submarines and Sukhoi–24s were designed by the Soviets to attack U.S. Navy forces—exactly what the Iranians appear to have in mind. Much of the other new purchases seem designed to disrupt shipping and U.S. naval routes through Gulf waters. The U.S. can only regard such a force as a threat: to oil tankers vital to Western economies, and to America's ability to reinforce its allies in the Gulf in the event of a crisis from any source.[1] In addition, Iran's military build-up could be laying the basis for a future capability to project power across the Persian Gulf, which would require an Iranian ability to deny Gulf access to the U.S. Navy.

• *The U.S. and a number of its allies seem to be in the process of trimming their worldwide strength.* While the U.S. will continue to have more than sufficient force to counter any Iranian thrust against its neighbors, it may not be able to keep many forces in the region (whether stationed permanently or visiting periodically). Iran could therefore more readily make a show of force designed to intimidate. Also, because a large American commitment of forces would occupy a significant share of global America's trimmed-down military, Washington is likely to be more reluctant to get involved in the event of threats or ambiguous developments.

• *The West may be missing its best opportunity to arrest Iran's military build-up* since the most effective moment that Western pressure can limit the build-up is precisely at the time that the orders have been placed, not after contracts have been signed or armaments have been built. Enough information is available for high-level policymakers to raise the matter with foreign leaders. Iran's submarine purchase from Russia illustrates this point. By the time Russia was ready to deliver the submarines to Iran, Pentagon officials were well informed about the progress of the submarine program. Due to the long

---

[1] Iran's acquisition of sea-denial weapons makes the Iranian-Sudanese alliance particularly troubling. Were Iran to move submarines or Sukhoi-24s to Sudan, it could threaten shipping on both sides of the Arabian peninsula.

lag period between when the order was first placed and
September 22, 1992, when the first Russian-built sub left for
Iran, Russian Foreign Minister Andrei Kozyrev did not take
Acting Secretary of State Eagleburger's request to block the sale
very seriously. Good intelligence and early action is not
necessarily a guarantee of success. The U.S. had been well
informed for some time about Iran's submarine program;
indeed, Admiral Sheafer testified about it to Congress in early
1992. Reportedly, the U.S. requested Saudi Arabia to offer to pay
Russia a higher price for the subs, but nothing came of the
request.[1]

• *Iran's defense budget is difficult to analyze.* This analysis
has concentrated on weapons purchases rather than on the
defense budget since Iran's distorted economy makes it nearly
impossible to compare Iran's military budget with that of other
countries. For instance, the 413 billion rials allocated in 1991-92
for training, technical research, and arms purchases would
translate into $5.9 billion at the official exchange rate but only
$295 million at the floating exchange rate used for most
transactions.[2] Both exchange rates are completely legal. The
reality is that a portion of the 413 billion rials was used for
foreign purchases. The armed forces were allowed to buy
foreign exchange at the cheap official rate, while the rest of the
rials were used to pay salaries and purchase goods and services
in Iran, where costs are close to Western levels when
translated at the floating rate. The overall defense budget is
dominated by salaries and local purchases, so it is not
meaningful to translate that budget into dollars at the official
rate. The best way to understand Iran's military might is to
concentrate on the equipment it possesses and attempts to
acquire, the number of soldiers it has under arms, and how
well it can use and integrate the new weapons into its existing
forces.

---

[1] *Ibid.* and *Washington Post*, October 1, 1992 and October 30, 1992.

[2] A point nicely developed by Scheherazade Daneshkhu, "Iran Presses on
with Campaign to Rebuild its Military Might," *Financial Times*, February
6, 1992.

NUCLEAR INTENTIONS

Much concern has been expressed recently about Iran's nuclear intentions. The Israel Defense Forces' (IDF) Intelligence Chief Uri Saguy, speaking on Israel Radio on June 8, 1992, said, "In my estimation if nobody stops the Iranians, they will be able to develop their own independent nuclear capability in eight to ten years."[1] CIA Director Robert Gates testified before the Senate Committee on Governmental Affairs that, "We have good reason to believe that Iran is pursuing collaborative arrangements with other would-be special weapons developers in the region" and that Iran is engaged in an "across the board effort" to develop its military and defense industries, including weapons of mass destruction.[2]

Iran has sent mixed signals about its intentions for developing nuclear weapons. A storm of publicity was generated by Deputy President Ataollah Mohajerani's statement on October 23, 1991 that, "If Israel should be allowed to have nuclear facilities, then Muslim states too should be allowed to have the same." Iranian Atomic Energy Organization (IAEO) officials rushed to deny that Iran intended to acquire nuclear weapons.[3] But statements on the subject by political leaders remain less than categorical. Ayatollah Khamenei, for example, in an address to reserves on July 1992, said: "You are mistaken if you think that the strength of the Islamic Republic lies in obtaining or manufacturing an atomic bomb... The power of the Islamic system ... is the power of faith of the Hezbollahi forces."[4]

Iranian leaders have vigorously defended Iran's long-standing civilian nuclear program. An American-supplied 5-

---

[1] *Mideast Mirror,* June 9, 1992.

[2] R. Jeffrey Smith, *Washington Post,* March 16, 1992.

[3] Mohajerani, who is also the IAEO Director, said that "Iran is not after nuclear arms. On the contrary, it believes such lethal arms in the region should be destroyed." *Iran Focus,* December 1991.

[4] *FBIS-NES*-92-135, July 14, 1992, pp. 49-50. See also *Washington Post,* November 17, 1992.

MW research reactor and an active IAEO were in place before the Revolution. The Shah signed contracts for six nuclear power plants and provided several billion dollars to finance France's uranium enrichment program. While these plans were shelved after the Revolution in 1979 and the IAEO operated on a low scale in the early 1980s, Iran's nuclear program was revitalized in the late 1980s under the leadership of publicity-seeking Deputy President Reza Amirollahi, who also served as head of the IAEO. The 1992-93 foreign exchange budget allocated $80 million for the IAEO.[1]

The main element in the IAEO's plans during the 1980s was completion of a nuclear power plant at Bushehr, a city on the coast of the Persian Gulf, by Kraft Werke Union (KfW), a German company. Under the 1976 contract, KfW was to build two 3,765 MW water pressure units eighteen km southwest of Bushehr.[2] By the time the Revolution forced a hiatus, 85 percent of the construction work and 65 percent of the mechanical and electrical work was done. When Iran wanted to resume the work, KfW refused, first citing danger during the war with Iraq, then concerns about the safety with which Iran would operate the plant; Iran charged that the real barrier was political. KfW and Iran submitted a claim for damages to an international arbitration panel, which ordered KfW to pay for maintenance of the unfinished facility and to ship thousands of tons of manuals, components, and nuclear fuel (the fuel was never sent, but 28,000 tons of material were).[3] The facility was bombed several times during the Iran-Iraq War, and it is generally thought that completion would require more than $1 billion dollars, and possibly as much as $3 billion.

As part of its campaign to gain approval for completion of the Bushehr plant, Iran has scrupulously cooperated with the International Atomic Energy Agency (IAEA). Indeed, since

---

[1] *Resalat*, April 15, 1992.

[2] From "Brief History of the Bushehr Nuclear Power Plants" prepared by the IAEO, *Jomhuri Islami*, August 1, 1992, as printed in *Akhbaar*, August 1, 1992.

[3] IRNA, March 4, 1991, as printed in *FBIS-NES*-91-45, March 5, 1991.

there was no radioactive material on site, Islamic Iran repeatedly invited the IAEA to inspect its facilities, including the as yet uncompleted Bushehr nuclear power plant which was not subject to IAEA requirements. It seems clear that Iran wanted to secure IAEA condemnation of Iraqi attacks on the Bushehr plant, similar to the IAEA condemnation of the Israeli raid on the Iraqi reactor at Osiraq. Following up on its normal program of inspections (the last was in November 1991),[1] the IAEA made a more extensive inspection in February 1992. Iran cooperated fully, permitting inspection of three sites not subject to IAEA controls: the uranium-mining site in Saghand (found to be five to seven years from operation, with no signs of the rumored uranium concentration plant), the Chinese-supplied calutron in Isfahan (found suitable only for producing stable isotopes of zinc for pharmaceutical purposes), and a facility near Moaalem Kalayeh, said by the Iranian opposition group (the Mojahedin) to be a key facility (found to be a motel-sized retreat for training and recreation).[2] This was the first time that the IAEA had inspected the facility though the country had not listed the facility as one subject to IAEA inspection.

Iran continues to state its willingness to cooperate with the IAEA. For instance, the deputy director of IAEO, Haji Azim, in criticizing the German government for not completing the Bushehr nuclear power plant, argued, "We have stated frequently that IAEA inspectors may be positioned at the power plant and that the Islamic Republic of Iran would pay the cost [for the inspections]."[3] In this context, the onus is on Western nations to identify Iranian sites that deserve IAEA inspection.

The record of cooperation with the IAEA would be more reassuring were that agency more effective. The IAEA failed to detect Iraq's multi-billion dollar effort to develop nuclear weapons, in large part because the agency depended entirely on the government in question for all of its information about nuclear programs. The IAEA had no means to solicit or

---

[1] Daneshkhu, "Iran Presses on," *Financial Times*, February 6, 1992.

[2] Michael Wise, "Atomic Team Reports on Iran Probe," *Washington Post*, February 15, 1992.

[3] Tehran Radio, August 2, 1992, as printed in *Akhbaar*, August 2, 1992.

evaluate information about possible treaty-violating activities, either from nuclear industry sources or from government intelligence agencies. Until such time as the IAEA develops a considerable capacity to ferret out treaty violations, it will be difficult to take seriously an IAEA clean bill of health.[1]

Concerns about Iran's nuclear weapons program have been heightened by its vigorous efforts to acquire nuclear power plants. In March 1990, Iran and the Soviet Union signed an agreement in principle for the sale of two 440 MW plants; the deal was finalized in September 1992.[2] During Rafsanjani's visit to Beijing in that month, he announced that agreement had been reached on the construction of a 330 MW nuclear power plant.[3] Since the Chinese had been expected to sell two reactors to Iran, some speculated that the sale of only one was in fact a Chinese move to reduce possible American opposition to the deal.[4] While Iran denied that the deal had any military implications, it was Iranian Defense Minister Torkan who accompanied Rafsanjani to Beijing, who officially announced the deal.

Furthermore, Iran has not given up on the Bushehr plant. Reza Amirollahi, Iran's Vice-President and head of the IAEO, and who continues vigorous efforts on a variety of fronts towards this end, said that "We would like to complete the Bushehr project as soon as possible."[5] During the visit of a

---

[1] For a recent account of how Saddam Hussein has been able to outwit the IAEA, see Gary Milhollin, "The New Arms Race: The Iraqi Bomb," *New Yorker*, February 1, 1993.

[2] Tehran Radio, March 7, 1990, as printed in *Akhbaar*, March 7, 1990; *New York Times*, September 24, 1992.

[3] Elaine Sciolino, *New York Times*, September 11, 1992. The negotiations had been underway for some months and had been extensively reported in Iran, e.g., *Abrar*, "Iran and China have Agreed to Erection of Nuclear Power Plant," August 1, 1992, translated in *Akhbaar*, August 1, 1992. There are also reports that Iran negotiated to purchase a research reactor from China in 1990 or 1991.

[4] *Iran Times*, September 18, 1992.

[5] In a Vienna press conference after visiting the IAEA; Tehran IRNA, February 26, 1992, as printed in *FBIS-NES*-92-041, March 2, 1992.

Siemens official to Tehran, several newspapers carried on a vigorous campaign for blackballing German firms until such time as the Bushehr power plant was finished.[1] Siemens director Von Pierrer apologized, "The Bushehr power plant question is a sad story which in addition to annoying Iranians has upset Siemens' employees... The German government should issue the license for the completion of the Bushehr nuclear power plant..."[2]

Iran's persistent interest in nuclear power plants is difficult to explain unless it is part of a plan to acquire nuclear weapons. Nuclear power plants make no economic sense for Iran, which has the world's second largest reserves of natural gas—an energy source which is difficult to sell and therefore makes more sense for domestic use. Generating electricity from natural gas is easy and requires a low capital investment, whereas nuclear power plants require an investment of billions of dollars in foreign exchange, capital Iran does not have. Sounder economic policies could save Iran at least half of the $2 billion a year it plans to spend on new power plants: raising the artificially cheap price of electricity would reduce demand,[3] and better maintenance of existing plants would increase the utilization rate from the abysmal 36 percent in 1989-90.[4]

The partially-built Bushehr nuclear power plant, however, is a plausible exception. A new power plant is needed in the mid-Gulf coast area where the plant is located, and the cost of completing the plant may be only slightly higher than that of building a gas plant from scratch. But Iran has clearly

---

[1] E.g., *Jomhuri Islami*'s editorial on August 2, 1992 was entitled "Siemens' Place is on Black List."

[2] Tehran Radio, August 3, 1992, as printed in *Akhbaar*, August 3, 1992.

[3] The Deputy Energy Minister reported in July 1992 that electricity costs 10 rials per kilowatt/hour, equal to .7 cents. The cost, excluding capital charges, was 14 rials (*Ettela'at*, July 9, 1992 as printed in *Akhbaar*, July 9, 1992).

[4] From a system with capacity of 16,619 million watts, 57,712 million kwh were generated and 39,965 million kwh were sold to customers (Chamber of Commerce, as printed in *Akhbaar*, May 18, 1991).

signaled that its nuclear ambitions do not stop with one plant. In addition, the Iranians have taken peculiar steps that are hard to explain unless they have an interest in developing a complete nuclear complex, such as lending $17 million to the International Center of Theoretical Physics in Italy[1] and signing an accord with Czechoslovakia for nuclear experts and uranium industry equipment.[2]

Iran's behavior demonstrates a fundamental flaw in the Non-Proliferation Treaty (NPT). The NPT is based on a bargain: in return for forsaking the development of nuclear weapons, the non-weapon states are guaranteed they will be given access to peaceful uses of nuclear technology. The IAEA exists not only to monitor for clandestine nuclear bomb programs but also to facilitate the spread of nuclear technology for peaceful uses. While the NPT bargain may have seemed reasonable when it was thought that nuclear power would become a preferred way to generate electricity, it no longer makes sense since nuclear power is rarely economical. There is no reason to believe that Iran or other energy rich states are developing nuclear power industries for peaceful purposes; therefore the IAEA should not be under any obligation to provide nuclear technology to such states. The wisest policy is that being followed by all major industrial states: to pay lip service to the NPT while blocking transfer of any nuclear technology to Iran.

Rumors have surfaced of a more immediate nuclear threat from Iran. *Al-Ahram* reported on October 13, 1991 that five tactical nuclear missiles had been transferred to Iran. A number of similar stories appeared that fall.[3] In March 1992, General Viktor Samoliv, in charge of disarmament matters on the CIS general staff, told Western visitors that three to six warheads were missing. On April 30, 1992, the *European* reported that, based on sources in Russia's Foreign Intelligence Service, two tactical nuclear artillery shells had been stolen

---

[1] *MEED*, December 13, 1991.

[2] As part of a $300 million trade pact; *Abrar*, May 22, 1989, as printed in *Akhbaar*, May 22, 1989.

[3] Timmerman, *Weapons of Mass Destruction*.

from the test range at Semipalatinsk and sold to Iranians. At a conference in Rome on June 15-16, 1992, Kazakh deputy Olzhas Sulejmanov, founder of the Nevada-Semipalatinsk Association, said three nuclear shells had been missing but had been found at the bottom of 600 meter mine shafts in Semipalatinsk where they had been readied for testing.

Der Spiegel reported a Soviet "nuclear expert was working as a street cleaner in Beersheba when former colleagues from Alma Ata approached him and persuaded him to move to Tehran. A complete research team from Kazakhstan is reportedly working there."[1] Such reports make for sensational journalism, but there has been little concrete evidence to back them up.

Rumor mills aside, the West needs to formulate a clear policy about the transfer of nuclear weapons and nuclear weapon technology from Kazakhstan to Iran. The foundation of that policy should be to hold both Alma Ata and Moscow fully and jointly responsible for any transfer that occurs. The weapons and weapon complexes are not under the effective control of the Kazakh government; Russia calls the shots. It is the responsibility of Moscow, as much as of Alma Ata, to ensure that personnel with special skills are kept track of and that security over weapons is maintained.

At present, Iran's conventional military is weak and will remain so for some years, until weapon systems on order can be delivered and soldiers can be trained to use and maintain these weapons. However, Iran is pursuing military capabilities specifically designed to attack U.S. forces, especially a sea denial capability that could hinder American access to Saudi Gulf ports in the event of an emergency when time may be of the essence. There is also reason to believe that Iran's nuclear energy program is a prelude to or cover for a nuclear weapons program.

The best time to forestall these threatening developments— the sea denial capability and the nuclear program—is when they are still on the drawing board rather than when they are close to being *faits accomplis*; in other words, the time to act is now, not the late 1990s. Furthermore, Iran's military could

---

[1] *Der Spiegel*, July 20, 1992, p. 117.

prove to be a more immediate threat were Iran to construct an alliance with one or more regional states.

III POTENTIAL IRANIAN THREATS TO WESTERN INTERESTS

Iran gives every indication of seeking both material and ideological reasons to confront the West, and it may have the military means to pose a considerable problem to its neighbors which are allied to the West. The challenges from Iran could take any of four general forms. It could try to dominate Persian Gulf oil, anchor a rejectionist front against Israel, merge Middle Eastern and South Asian conflicts, or challenge Turkey.

DOMINATING PERSIAN GULF OIL

Persian nationalism and Iran's quest for resources could lead Iran to take aggressive actions to dominate the Gulf oil output. No matter what form that domination may take, it would be against American interests. As the world's largest consumer and importer of oil, the U.S. cannot be indifferent when one state attempts to wrest control of the 70 percent of the world's oil reserves which lie along the Persian Gulf littoral. Any state that dominated Gulf oil could dictate the price within a broad band, either driving the price so low that U.S. domestic output would be rendered uneconomic, or raising the price to a level that would drain billions out of the U.S. economy.

The U.S. would be particularly vulnerable in the short term, and even in the longer run; the cost of instituting conservation measures and developing alternative energy sources would be a difficult burden, and the U.S. would bear more of a burden than many other Western countries which are better insulated from rises in the price of oil by heavy fuel taxes. Not only would domination of Persian Gulf oil by Iran pose a heavy economic burden on the U.S., it would evoke a justifiable concern that an antagonistic Iran could use its domination of Gulf oil to blackmail the U.S. for political purposes, raising the oil price and restricting output well beyond what would be justified on an economic rationale alone.

Would Iran dare to move to assert control over the oil fields, having seen the potency of the U.S. reaction to the Iraqi attempt to increase its share of Gulf oil? The answer depends in part on the precise lesson the Iranian leaders drew from Desert Storm. Possibly the lesson was that while the U.S. can administer powerful punishment, it lacks the staying power to achieve its ends—Desert Storms are awesome in might, but pass quickly. Howard Teicher warns, "The failure of Desert Storm to reap a political victory and remove Hussein has encouraged Iran to gradually, but deliberately, intensify" efforts to test its power in the Gulf, such as its moves against the UAE over Abu Musa Island.[1]

The U.S. military will be able to dominate the Gulf for as long as it has the will to do so. However, the reduction in the size of U.S. forces planned for the mid-1990s means that a commitment to the Gulf would require earmarking a sizable proportion of global U.S. forces for a potential Gulf deployment. This is especially true if the American presence is to continue at its 1992 level with substantial deployment of planes in Saudi Arabia, periodic aircraft carrier visits to Gulf waters, and occasional ground exercises in Kuwait. Nevertheless, the fact remains that Iran cannot dominate the Gulf unless the U.S. decides to let it.

If American inaction provides Iran with an opening, Iran has a variety of options available to acquire control over the region's oil reserves. Rafsanjani is too clever to attempt a blatant Saddam-style grab: a Saddam-like invasion of Saudi Arabia is implausible because, for the foreseeable future, Iran lacks a sufficient military capability to invade and seize any of the large Gulf states. Furthermore, based on the experience of the Iran-Iraq War, Iran prefers to rely on clever pressure tactics.

---

[1] Howard Teicher, "Is There a Saddam Hussein Lurking Behind Tehran's Moderate Face?", *Los Angeles Times*, April 26, 1992.

For example, although Iran obeyed the letter of an American warning not to block the Straits, it was able to achieve much the same goal of impeding shipping by laying low-tech and plausibly-deniable mines, which the U.S. Navy was ill-equipped to counter.

The small Gulf sheikdoms are a particularly vulnerable point. Iran could use threats of terrorism against the small states, perhaps drawing on the large ethnic Iranian communities and/or Iranian temporary laborers in Kuwait, Bahrain, Qatar, and the UAE. Iran could also attempt to dominate the Persian Gulf waters, insisting on a larger share of offshore oil output and/or transit fees from tankers.

Iran may not need to use brute force for these purposes; instead, it might try to form an alliance with Saudi Arabia, to divide the smaller states of the Gulf between themselves. It would be inappropriate to assume that the relationship between the U.S. and Saudi Arabia will always remain closer than that between Iran and Saudi Arabia. Iran and Saudi Arabia share a common commitment to the primacy of Islam in politics which could, at some point, overcome their very different concepts of Islam. In the spring and summer 1992, at the same time that Iran was pressuring Kuwait, Qatar, and the UAE, Iran made conciliatory gestures towards Riyadh. Reversing years of hard politicking about the *haj*, Iran went out of its way to maintain a low profile. Ayatollah Khamenei issued a *fatwa* on May 24 forbidding the celebration of Shi'i rituals which annoy Saudis, such as kissing Muhammad's grave. Iran's *haj* leader Mohammad Mahammadi Reyshahri described the message of Iran as one of "unity, fraternity, and friendship under the banner of monotheism."[1]

Iran could direct pressure toward several goals, each of which would serve to secure higher income for Iran from Gulf oil. One technique would be to secure a large quota for itself while insisting that the other Gulf states limit their output, which would increase the price. For instance, if Iran could secure a production output of five mbd and limit the other Gulf

---

[1] *MEED*, June 5, 1992, p. 14. On the other hand, as soon as a border dispute erupted between Saudi Arabia and one of its smaller neighbors, Qatar, Tehran leaped to the side of Riyadh's opponents.

states to seven mbd, oil prices could rise to $30 a barrel;[1] Iran's income in this scenario would be $24.7 billion a year. The high price would probably erode within five to seven years, as high prices encourage conservation and the development of oil fields elsewhere, including in the U.S. But Iran's interests would be served by the temporarily high price: since its reserves are being depleted, it does not have the potential to expand output and therefore does not have as much reason to worry about long-term erosion of oil's share in the world energy market. Other methods Iran could use to achieve the same end of maximizing its revenue from Gulf oil include demanding a larger share of offshore oil (an increasingly important part of Gulf oil output), and pressuring other states to "invest" in Iran, in what would amount to little more than disguised robbery.

Another scenario in which Iran could maximize its oil income would be for it to take advantage of the de facto partition of Iraq to exercise control over the south—site of about 10 percent of the world's oil reserves—and thus add three mbd to Iran's oil output within five years. In the event of Kurdish autonomy cum independence, Iran could seek to dominate either all of what remained of Iraq, which would be at least two-thirds Shi'i, or just the south, which would be almost entirely Shi'i.[2] The Iraqi Shi'a might not welcome such Iranian influence, but they may have little alternative. if they wish to control all of Iraq, or at least a southern enclave, they need allies. Iran may be more a more willing and a more acceptable alternative than the West for this purpose. In the event the takeover took the form of an insurrection rather than a coup, Iran would have a wide range of instruments with which to intervene. The establishment of an Iranian safe

---

[1] That price could emerge if oil output from the former Soviet Union continues to decline, the world economy recovers from its current stagnation, and concerns about the greenhouse effect do not lead to significant new taxes or controls on oil use.

[2] Regardless of whether the Kurdish areas become fully autonomous, Tehran could also seek a temporary alliance of convenience with Baghdad, fueled by a common hatred of the West and a common desire to acquire more income from Gulf oil. This possibility is discussed in the last section of this paper.

haven for rebels would encourage more rebel risk-taking and reduce their concerns about retaliation against their families. Provision of supplies (humanitarian or military) could turn a one-time rebellion into an on-going affair. Insertion of a communications and intelligence network could convert isolated local rebellions into a coordinated threat to Baghdad's control.

It is difficult to see either the West or Saudi Arabia being prepared to wage a major war against such a development. Iran could, after all, plausibly claim in the court of world opinion to be representing the will of the area's residents. In any autonomous southern Iraq, Shi'ite religious leaders would probably predominate, given that Saddam has eliminated nearly all other potential rivals. The long history of close ties between Iranian and Iraqi Shi'ite religious leaders would lend credence to Iran as the partner of choice for the Iraqi Shi'ite leaders. Indeed, there are almost certain to be some leaders among the Iraqi Shi'a who would genuinely welcome Iranian intervention. Iran could create a puppet state rather than annexing the region. All these factors would make the situation morally ambiguous, very different from the cut-and-dry case of the Iraqi invasion of Kuwait.

A Shi'ite entity in southern Iraq could be a considerable asset to Tehran. It could quickly be made into a self-sustaining area economically, producing over a million barrels of oil a day which could be readily exported directly via the narrow Iraqi Gulf coast or via the adjoining Iranian network. Furthermore, it would provide Iran with a land route through which it could project power vis-a-vis the Gulf monarchies, and which could serve as direct invasion route.

ANCHORING A REJECTIONIST FRONT AGAINST ISRAEL

Iranian leaders of all stripes firmly reject the existence of the Jewish state, for accepting it would mean the abandonment of its carefully nurtured claim to leadership of militant Islam. As detailed above, Iran's leaders are strongly opposed to the current Arab-Israeli peace process and have tried in vain to derail the talks. Iranian opposition so far worked primarily through terrorist groups, especially Hamas and Hezbollah. The disturbing prospect exists that the radical anti-Western forces throughout the Middle East may be coalescing in opposition to the peace process.

However troubling to the tranquillity of everyday life in Israel, the radical bloc's terrorist attacks would not necessarily imperil the peace process. Nevertheless, the situation would change sharply if the radicals under Iran's leadership were able to attract one of the states bordering Israel, which in practice means Syria. President Hafez al-Assad may want an alternative in case peace talks do not go well; he is clever enough to always have an alternative ready in case his current path runs into a dead end. Were he to opt for a radical stance, Assad could use an Iranian-inspired rejectionist front to provide him with ideological and military backing. Iran could play the 'bad cop' to Syria's 'good cop' in a coordinated one-two game with the West.

The Tehran-Damascus Connection

A Syrian-Iranian alliance makes sense on several fronts. For one thing, both governments are dominated by non-Sunnis. Some Sunnis have long feared a grand Shi'ite empire stretching from Lebanon through Syria (many Sunnis regard Syria's Alawis as essentially Shi'ites in disguise) through Iraq to Iran. On a more prosaic level, Syria and Islamic Iran have long been allied on the basis of common opposition to the West. After difficulties over Lebanon in 1990-91, the relationship has been patched up. As Tony Walker wrote in the *Financial Times*,

> Syria and Iran have boosted significantly their defense cooperation since the end of the Gulf crisis, prompting western suspicions that the two are actively collaborating in securing weapons of mass destruction, notably missiles... A Western attache in Damascus described the combination of Iran and Syria as 'potentially very dangerous.' He said the 'strange marriage' could pose 'the next century's threat to the Middle East.'... Another western official said there were also indications that Syria and Iran were building stronger defense links with China

and Pakistan, and this was 'troubling' in the light of fears of the further spread of nuclear technology.[1]

One past constraint on a Syrian-Iranian alliance was that Syria had to give priority to relations with its funders in Riyadh and Moscow, but that situation has changed substantially in the last two years. The dissolution of the Soviet Union and the consequent decline in aid is only part of the reason for this change; Syria has undergone a little-noted economic reversal that could lead to a sea-change in Middle Eastern power relations—Syria has become an oil exporter.

Figured at a price of $18 per barrel, Syrian oil production in 1992 was worth $3.3 billion.[2] To put this in perspective, Syria's aid from all sources—whether civilian or military, from the West, Arabs, or Soviet Union—was never as much as $3 billion in a year.

In other words, Syria now earns more money from oil than it ever received in aid. This fact will enable Damascus to approach Tehran as a potential strategic partner, not as a mendicant who will take Iran's side if provided with enough money (Iran used to ship oil worth several hundred million dollars per year to Syria during the Iran-Iraq war either free or at a significantly reduced price).

Syrian oil income will increase in strategic significance in the future. The effect of the oil income will increase as a larger share of each dollar in exports flows into the government coffers; to date, much of the export revenues has been retained by the oil companies to recover the exploration and development costs. Syrian government revenue from oil exports may have been less than $1 billion in 1991 but could rise to over $2 billion in 1993.[3] Oil income will continue to

---

[1] Tony Walker, "Syria-Iran Defense Links Arouse Western Suspicion," *Financial Times*, March 6, 1992.

[2] In 1992 Syria produced 500,000 b/d: 350,000 b/d of high quality (light, low sulfur) crude produced by the Al-Furat Petroleum Company and 150,000 b/d of low quality crude produced by the Syrian Petroleum Company. *MEED*, September 18, 1992, p. 17.

[3] Author's calculation, based on domestic oil consumption of 200,000 b/d and a typical structure for repaying exploration and development costs.

become more significant because of active Syrian development of additional oil fields.[1] Syria may well achieve its aim of producing one mbd by the year 2000.

Syrian oil income could have an immense impact on the region's strategic balance. Oil production translates directly into government revenue, which means that Hafez al-Assad will, for the first time, have a guaranteed means to finance his military machine under his control. He will no longer be dependent on the largesse of either Riyadh or Moscow. Furthermore, Assad will have hard currency at precisely the moment when his main arms suppliers, the successor states of the former Soviet Union, are eager to raise dollars by any means and more than ready to sell arms, the one product it has stocked in abundance and which it has ample capacity to produce. To be sure, Soviet equipment is not equal to what Israel possesses, but the sheer volume that Syria could field would require a continually high state of Israeli readiness.[2]

Furthermore, with Syria in a position to pay in hard currency, it might well secure access to Western electronics with which it can upgrade the Soviet weapons "platforms"— that is, the basic vehicle (whether a land vehicle, plane, or ship) on which the various weapons and electronic guidance and communication gear are mounted. In the new international environment, a number of Western firms are looking at ways to marry their systems with Soviet platforms for customers, such as the German Air Force which now uses MiG-29s. The blend of Soviet platforms with Western electronics may become nearly as potent as Western equipment, if the West continues with plans to use existing basic weapon systems while canceling large-scale development of major new weapon systems.

---

[1] The Deir ez-Zor Petroleum Company (a joint venture between the Syrian Petroleum Company and Elf Aquitaine) will produce 60,000 b/d of high quality crude by mid-1994, and as much as 120,000 b/d by mid-1996. The Al Furat Petroleum Company is also expanding capacity by 50,000 b/d for 1993, and has plans to expand even more. *MEED*, September 11, 1992, p. 21, and September 18, 1992, p. 17.

[2] See the analysis in Michael Eisenstadt, *Arming for Peace? Syria's Elusive Quest for "Strategic Parity,"* Policy Paper No. 31 (Washington, D.C.: The Washington Institute for Near East Policy, 1992).

A Syrian-Iranian rejectionist front would be supported by several other Arab states. It would of course be endorsed by Lebanon, which has effectively become little more than western Syria. Iraq would lend at least rhetorical support to the rejectionist cause, simply because it would by nature be anti-Western. However, so long as the current regime retains power in Baghdad, its long-standing rivalry with Damascus and Tehran would prevent any practical aid to the rejectionist front. In the unlikely event that Iraq no longer enjoyed sovereignty over Kurdistan and was allied with Iran, the power of the rejectionists would be increased because of their access to a land bridge through which Iranian forces could reinforce Syria.[1]

A more likely scenario would be support for a rejectionist front from the North African fringes of the Arab world where Iran has been active. The most important Iranian beach-head in the entire Arab world has been in Sudan, which would provide rhetorical support to a rejectionist front. If the FIS, a militant fundamentalist group, had been able to take over Algeria during the elections in Algeria of December 1991 and January 1992, it too would have lent propaganda support. In any event the FIS would have been able to do little of any practical significance.

Even if a new rejectionist front were confined to Syria and Iran and received tacit support from Lebanon and Sudan, it is possible that it would possess enough military strength to make Syria think that it could take provocative steps without worrying too much about Israeli reaction. The result might not be another war, but the tensions would lead to a renewed arms race that the region can ill afford.

MERGING SOUTH ASIAN AND MIDDLE EASTERN CONFLICTS

One of the more frightening, but fortunately not too probable, forms that an Iranian challenge to the West could take would be a strategic alliance with Pakistan. What makes

---

[1] The rejectionist front would benefit if a "post-Kurdish" Iraq were either (1) united and allied to Iran, or (2) divided into a Shi'i south allied to Iran and a Sunni center which would fall under the influence of Damascus.

such an alliance worrisome is that Pakistan has nuclear weapons; Pakistani Foreign Secretary Shahryar Khan admits that his country has the components and the know-how to assemble at least one nuclear bomb, though he claimed Pakistan had not assembled such a bomb.[1] In the event of a Pakistani-Iranian alliance, Iran might be able to gain access to a Pakistani-built nuclear bomb, though Pakistan would be much more likely to provide nuclear technology than actual weapons. At the least, were Pakistan and Iran to form an alliance, the West would have to worry whether a confrontation with Iran could escalate to the nuclear level. That worry could by itself be a deterrent against Western action.

An alliance with Iran holds numerous attractions for Pakistan. Islamabad feels isolated in the world: its alliance with the U.S. has ended with the resolution of the anti-communist war in Afghanistan and the fading U.S. concern about the Indian-Soviet alliance (which has, in any case, become much weaker). Meanwhile, Pakistan faces a serious security threat from India, a state which in the 1980s invaded or blockaded four of its neighbors (Nepal, Bangladesh, Sri Lanka, and the Maldives).

In the event of a confrontation with India, an alliance with Iran would increase Pakistan's strategic depth. Access to Iranian bases would allow Pakistan to operate out of range of possible Indian attack. Cooperation with Iran could also help further Pakistan's ambitions in Central Asia; Pakistan feels an alliance with Central Asian states would do much to isolate India from renewed friendship with Russia. From an ideological point of view, an alliance with Iran reinforces the somewhat shaky Islamic credentials of the Pakistani military. In addition, Iran has for centuries been a point of reference for Muslim intellectuals in the Indian sub-continent.

The major spokesman for a strategic Iranian-Pakistani alliance has been General Aslam Beg, the chief of staff in 1990-91.[2] In a speech on December 13, 1990—in the middle of

---

[1] R. Jeffrey Smith, "Pakistan can Build One Nuclear Device, Foreign Official Says," *Washington Post*, February 7, 1992.

[2] VIRI, March 25, 1990, in *Summary of World Broadcasts*, Me/0724/A/2, March 28, 1990, as cited in Shahram Chubin, "Iran and the Lessons of the Gulf War 1991."

the crisis over Kuwait—General Beg argued that Pakistan had to reduce reliance on the West and develop a new orientation:

> It would be difficult for us to try to stop aggression on our own. So, one aim of our policy should be to obtain support from friendly countries. In my opinion, it should not be difficult to cultivate friendship with Iran and Afghanistan. We have a lot in common with them in terms of geographic boundaries, history, and culture.[1]

Iranian-Pakistani cooperation has been building since Desert Storm. During his September 1991 visit to Tehran, President Ghulam Ishaq Khan of Pakistan, to date the only foreign dignitary to address Islamic Iran's parliament, "argued for cooperation among Muslim states for building an indigenous defense capability rather than buying security from outsiders."[2] Rafsanjani, in a speech delivered to the Pakistani Parliament in September 1992, called for closer cooperation between the two countries to resist "domineering arrogant power."[3] Reviewing the potential for Pakistani-Iranian ties, Shahram Chubin concludes, "A sort of 'pariah's international' cannot be excluded if the new world order turns out to be warmed-over pax Americana with UN trimmings."

However, a variety of factors serve to keep Iran and Pakistan apart. The tension within Pakistan over the country's Shi'ite minority (about 10 percent of the population) has been the object of discriminatory rulings in the course of the implementation of Islamic rule in Pakistan, and is sure to prove a difficult obstacle to overcome on the path toward Iranian-Pakistani cooperation.

Another source of Pakistani-Iranian tension is the future of Afghanistan. During the years of Soviet occupation, successive Pakistani governments spent much political capital and channeled many U.S.-provided dollars to support the movement led by Hekmatyar. The Pakistani government

---

[1] *Jang* (Karachi), December 14, 1990, as printed in *FBIS Joint Publications Research Service-NEA*-91-022, April 5, 1991.

[2] Salamat Ali, *Far Eastern Economic Review*, October 3, 1991, p. 29.

[3] *Financial Times*, September 8, 1992.

expected Hekmatyar would effectively control the Afghan government after the Soviet-backed regime collapsed. Instead, he has been the main loser in the new arrangements; he has been frozen out of the new government and his forces control little of the country's territory.[1] While Hekmatyar—and indeed the entire Pushtun traditional ruling elite to which Pakistan looks—have been marginalized, and several Persian-speakers hold key government posts. Having been a major actor over the years in the Afghani conflict, Pakistan is not pleased to find that, as the *Financial Times* reported, "Many countries have stuck their fingers into the Afghan pie during fourteen years of the civil war, but none has emerged with as much to show as Iran."

CHALLENGING TURKEY

Relations between Iran and Turkey have deteriorated badly over four issues, none of which are likely to improve in the next few years:

Challenge in Azerbaijan

President Abulfaz Elchibey of former Soviet Azerbaijan has referred to his country as "northern Azerbaijan," an open provocation to Iran which has three Azeri provinces in the northwest.[2] It is unclear how many Iranians identify themselves as Azeri, given the extent of intermarriage and fading ethnic consciousness. Estimates of the size of the Azeri population range from six million to fifteen million.[3] Some Azeris are well integrated into Iranian society; Ayatollah Khamenei, for example, has Azeri roots. But Iran has reason to worry about the loyalty of its Azeri population, which has not fully absorbed the dominant Persian culture. Despite a

---

[1] Colin Barraclough, *Financial Times*, May 14, 1992.

[2] *Iran Times*, July 10, 1992.

[3] The low estimate is based on the fact that 12 percent of Iran's fifty-nine million people live in the overwhelmingly Azeri provinces; the high estimate is based on the CIA estimate that 25 percent of Iran's population is Azeri (*World Factbook 1992*).

schooling system that is entirely in Persian, the 1986 Census reported that only 40 percent of those in East Azerbaijan province speak primarily Persian.[1] Ethnic consciousness may be increasing in the area: the fall 1992 decision to include Azeri word lists in the area's elementary school texts (with a promise to consider Azeri lessons in fall 1993) is a sharp departure from years of insistence that only Persian can be used in any transaction with the government.[2]

Iranians are well aware that Turkey will want to dominate independent Azerbaijan, not only because of ethnic ties, but as a means for better access to the Turkish-speaking areas of Central Asia (to reach those areas from Turkey requires going through Russia, Iran, or Azerbaijan). Iran cannot be pleased by the seconding to the new Azerbaijani armed forces of 150 Turkish retired officers above the rank of colonel, especially given that President Elchibey has called for the overthrow of the Iranian regime, calling it a "form of fascism that hides behind religion."[3]

Turkish relations with independent Azerbaijan immediately raise the issue of Armenian-Azeri relations. Turkey's common border with Azerbaijan is only five kilometers long, along the enclave of Nakchivan, an area separated from the rest of Azerbaijan by the territory of Armenia.[4] To reduce Turkish influence in Azerbaijan and to curb the power of Azerbaijan (i.e., to curb the danger it represents to Iranian Azerbaijan), Iran is tempted to support Christian Armenians against Muslim Azeris—an inclination increased by the historically good relations between Iran and ethnic Armenians, many of whom are prominent in Tehran business circles. Additionally, ethnic Armenians are guaranteed two seats in Iran's Majlis.

---

[1] *Iran Economic Bulletin*, as printed in *Akhbaar*, September 24, 1990.

[2] *Iran Times*, July 24, 1992.

[3] *Mideast Mirror*, November 13, 1992.

[4] Furthermore, Nakchivan's leader Gaydar Aliyev (former number three in the Soviet Communist Party) has developed close relations with Iran, leading to what appear to have been coup attempts against him by Elchibey.

Central Asia

Both Iran and Turkey claim a special role in Central Asia. Four of the Central Asian republics—Turkmenistan, Uzbekistan, Kazakhstan, and Kirghizstan—are inhabited largely by Turkic-speaking people. Uniting these peoples is the dream of pan-Turkism, long a force on the Turkish right. On the other hand, Iran regards the region as part of its natural sphere of influence, under Iranian domination for most of the last three millennia.[1]

Iran's leaders have been shocked at the explicitly anti-Islamist and anti-Iranian tone that the Turkish campaign for influence in the area has taken. Turkey has moved fast to offer its services, and to present itself as an example for the region: a Western-style economy which is both secular and heavily state-dominated. It has explicitly presented its activities as a counter to the influence of Iran and Islamic fundamentalists. Meanwhile, Uzbekistan has waged a major campaign to blame Iranian meddling for the civil war in Tadzhikistan, which it portrays as the product of Islamic fanatics.

The dangers of Iranian-inspired fundamentalism in Central Asia have been exaggerated. The region does indeed have a vigorous Islamist movement, but it is homegrown. The Islamists are not the principal factor behind the Tadzhikistan fighting, which is more about regional disputes and about whether the old communist elite can be displaced. To date, there is little reason to think that religion will be the driving force in future Iranian-Central Asian relations.

On the other hand, there are a host of opportunities for economic ties, which both sides have shown interest in developing. Central Asia needs to develop alternatives to routes through Russia for its foreign trade; simple geography gives Iran a tremendous advantage in this regard. It is only 600-1,000 miles across relatively flat country from Central Asia's economic heartland to the Iranian Persian Gulf port at Bandar

---

[1] For the region's history, see Renee Greusset, *The Empire of the Steppes: A History of Central Asia* (New Brunswick, New Jersey: Rutgers University Press, 1970). For more recent developments, see Martha Brill Olcott, "Central Asia's Post-Empire Polities," *Orbis*, Spring 1992.

Abbas. Turkey, on the other hand, has poor land routes to the region, all of which cross through other countries. As Western (principally U.S.) firms develop the extensive gas and oil reserves of Turkmenistan and Kazakhstan, the alternative trade routes are clearly Russia or Iran. Kazakhstan's President Nursultan Nazarbayev has announced that his country's oil will be exported in equal portions through each of these routes, to the disappointment of Turkey which had hoped for a role through a complicated route crossing under the Caspian Sea.[1]

Kurds

Turkey has periodically claimed that Iran provides cover for Kurdish Workers Party (PKK) rebels. In early September 1992, Iran forced two Turkish military planes to land in Iran, in what may have been related to a Turkish campaign against Kurdish rebels for which Turkey had mobilized 150,000 men along the border with Iran.[2] In mid-September 1992, Turkish Interior Minister Ismet Szegin flew to Iran, where he agreed with his Iranian counterpart, Abdollah Nuri, that Turkey would suppress Mojahedin operatives inside Turkey in return for Iran suppressing PKK operatives in Iran,[3] a deal confirmed during the subsequent visit to Tehran by Turkish Prime Minister Suleyman Demirel.

Islamists

Iran has supported the revival of Islamist tendencies in Turkey, ranging from the wearing of Islamic dress to public displays of religion. These tendencies are anathema to old-style Kemalists, who are strong in the military. The conflict is not acute at present, but it could well flare up, especially if Islamist currents grow in Turkey. The January 1993 murder of a prominent liberal Turkish journalist, Ugur Mumcu,

[1] *MEED*, December 7, 1992.

[2] *New York Times*, September 9, 1992. Iran denied Turkish claims that the PKK launched an attack from Iranian soil that killed ten Turkish soldiers; cf. *Kayhan Havayi*, September 9, 1992.

[3] *Iran Times*, September 18, 1992.

evidently by Iranian-backed Islamists, is an indication that Islamist currents may indeed be increasing.

Turkish-Iranian relations are not helped by increasing commercial competition. Whereas during the years of radical-provoked stagnation, Iran was a good market for Turkish producers, the limited Rafsanjani reforms have made Iranian products competitive in Turkish markets. Iranian agricultural produce and simple manufactured goods like washing powder captured an extensive share in the eastern Turkish market before controls were imposed.[1]

The net result of all these challenges is that Iran and Turkey could become strategic enemies. When Iranian Defense and Armed Forces Logistics Minister Ahmed Torkan reviewed how Iran's next Five Year Defense Plan would be affected by the changes in the world situation, he gave prominence to potential problems with Turkey.[2] Iranian newspapers gave prominent coverage to the prediction by Maher Kainak, a retired MIT (Turkish military intelligence) official, that Turkey will fight a war with Iran in the near future.[3]

The reason for the West to be concerned about an Iranian challenge to Turkey is not simply the existence of a formal obligation for common defense in the NATO treaty. The security guarantee to Turkey over the last forty years was based on the Soviet threat, which is no longer credible. But a new threat has appeared to both Turkey and the West. Both share a common interest in containing expansionist anti-Western Islamism. The West does not want to see the radical political vision of Islam spread into European Muslim communities. Europe's Muslims are found not only in the three majority Muslim nations on the European periphery (Albania, Bosnia-Herzegovina, and Turkey), but also in the

---

[1] *Jomhuri Islami*, March 29, 1992, as printed in *Akhbaar*, March 29, 1992.

[2] "We have to think of Turkey in another way, given its new strategy, and, in view of the new condition of the region, choose a more precise way. What is going on in Central Asia and in Turkey has completely changed the region's geopolitics and brought about new political threats in the region." Jam Number 4, as printed in *Akhbaar*, June 9, 1992.

[3] *Noqteh* (Istanbul), as printed in *Kayhan Havai*, August 19, 1992.

large Muslim communities in France, Germany, and Britain—each with more than a million Muslims. Turkey can play a vital role in counterbalancing any impulse in these communities towards radical Islam by demonstrating that a democratic secular government can indeed be successful in a country with a population of devout and practicing Muslims. An Iranian-led destabilization of Turkey would undermine the Turkish secular example and, more importantly, lead to a spectacular growth among the already worrisome Turkish fundamentalist forces present in large numbers in Western Europe (especially in Germany), as well as to Turkish anti-Western Islamic propagandists throughout the Balkans.

The risk of spreading anti-Western Islamism among European Muslims has grown because of unrest in the Balkans, where vicious Serbian nationalists seem determined to provoke a radical Islamic reaction by targeting their Bosnian opponents for being Muslim fanatics. The crude Serbian attacks on Islam, the vicious treatment of Bosnian Muslims, the weak response of European nations, and the rhetorical solidarity of radical Muslims with the Bosnian cause have created the impression among some European Muslims that they should count on radical Muslims, rather than European governments, to guarantee their most basic human rights. Iranian planes have been found to be shipping arms to Bosnia.[1] Ayatollah Khamenei, in a meeting with the Iranian organization for aid to Bosnia, "explained the Moslem nations' readiness to send forces to Bosnia-Herzegovina."[2] The Revolutionary Guards issued a statement, "The militant pasdars and mobilization men of the Pasdaran Corps are ready... to take steps under the command of the guardian of the world's Moslems, the Rev. Ayatollah Khamenei, to save the victimized Moslem people of Bosnia-Herzegovina and avenge the blood of defenseless children and women on the criminal Serbs."[3] *Le Monde* reported, "According to Iranian sources,

---

[1] Michael Gordon, "Iran Said to Send Arms to Bosnians," *New York Times*, September 10, 1992.

[2] Tehran Radio, October 12, 1992, as printed in *Akhbaar*, October 12, 1992.

[3] *Jomhuri Islami*, October 8, 1992, as printed in *Akhbaar*, October 8, 1992.

Tehran offers $600 per month to anyone ready to fight on the side of the Muslims in Bosnia-Herzegovina."[1]

Iran on its own lacks the means to present a short-term challenge to most of America's vital interests in the region. However, Iran could threaten Western interests were it to form a coalition with like-minded forces. Together with Syria, and aided by Palestinian and Lebanese extremists, Iran could construct a new anti-Israel rejectionist front. In conjunction with Sudan, Iran has already done much to penetrate the Sunni world and to aid domestic forces destabilizing the North African governments; were one of those governments to fall to Islamist factions, an anti-Western alliance could compete for the allegiance of Muslims in many countries. If Iran acted in conjunction with the PKK, it could cause trouble for Turkey (or for Turkey's ally Azerbaijan if Iran aided Armenia). In the unlikely, but not impossible, event that Iran formed an alliance with either Iraq or Pakistan, Iran could pose a threat to the free flow of oil from the Gulf.

None of these alliances are imminent, but all are within the realm of possibility. Iran seems to be pressing ahead on each front, and the chances that one of these scenarios will come to pass is therefore high enough to merit serious consideration.

---

[1] Afsane Bassirpour, *Le Monde*, November 18, 1992.

IV   WESTERN POLICY OPTIONS

Conflicting interests need not lead to irreconcilable conflict. Diplomacy provides many tools with which to respond to differences among nations. But the ability to avoid sharp conflict depends in part on correctly identifying the difference in interests and the effects of the policies adopted. In that spirit, let us consider the advantages and disadvantages of three Western policy alternatives towards Islamic Iran: bring Iran into the family of nations, apply carrots and sticks, and practice a policy of containment.

The goals of U.S. policy toward Iran are taken here to be essentially the geostrategic aims: preserving the free flow of oil from the Gulf, promoting Arab-Israeli peace, preventing the proliferation of weapons of mass destruction, protecting Americans from terrorism, and supporting allies against subversion. The U.S. also has a variety of humanitarian and idealistic goals which serve its long-term geostrategic interests by promoting a world of like-minded states: fostering democracy, protecting human rights (both for individuals and ethnic/religious minorities), encouraging free-market economies, and advancing ecologically sustainable development. It is assumed here that a dialogue on such issues with Iran will be difficult to achieve; the U.S. will thus not be able to significantly advance these interests and should concentrate on its geostrategic aims.

BRING IRAN INTO THE FAMILY OF NATIONS

The Clinton administration has been urged by some Iran-watchers to adopt a more conciliatory approach toward Tehran. Jerrold Green, for example, argued that, "It is time for the West to accept the Iranian Revolution while nudging Iran back into the global community where it belongs."[1] Japan and European governments have adopted this approach and are determined to work with the current Iranian government to the extent possible in the hopes of reinforcing moderate elements. A Tehran-based Western diplomat explained,

> As far as the European Community is concerned, the question is do we want to help pragmatists like Rafsanjani come out on top or not? The answer is that is in our interest to have a normal Iran, busily rebuilding its economy, not an aggressive Iran that feels isolated and abandoned.[2]

In particular, they are encouraging vigorous economic ties with Iran. This includes extending loans guaranteed by official credit agencies. The official export loan agencies of Germany, Japan, Italy, France, and Britain all compete for business with Iran. For instance, in November 1992, France's COFACE (the French equivalent of the American Export-Import Bank) agreed to guarantee a $360 million loan on favorable terms,[3] and Italy agreed to lend $100 million for small and medium industry.[4] Several Western countries have gone beyond short-term credits to finance the acquisition of heavy equipment with long-term loans. For instance, after a 17-year hiatus, Japan resumed foreign aid loans to Iran in

---

[1] Jerrold Green, "Iran's Foreign Policy: Between Enmity and Conciliation," *Current History*, January 1993, p. 16.

[2] Youssef Ibrahim, "Rebounding Iranians are Striving for Regional Leadership in Gulf," *New York Times*, November 7, 1992.

[3] *Janah-e Eqtesad*, November 9, 1992, as printed in *Akhbaar*, November 12, 1992. The favorable term was that the loan was not guaranteed by the government or central bank of Iran.

[4] *Keyhan*, November 9, 1992, as printed in *Akhbaar*, November 9, 1992.

November 1992 lending $280 million for a hydroelectric project.[1]

Furthermore, high technology goods are flowing to Iran. German "government officials are approving 80 percent of applications by German companies seeking to export sensitive civilian high technology to Iran."[2] The Japanese government has argued that Iran should be permitted access to high technology exports despite the possible military use of some of these exports. Foreign Minister Michio Watanabe argued, "We cannot agree 100 percent with the United States because our ties [with Iran] go a long way back and are different from Iran-U.S. relations."[3] *Yomiuri Shimbun* editorialized, "Japan's efforts to guide Iran into cooperation with Western nations benefit the world community... Resuming yen credits to Iran... will help reality-oriented political forces in Iran."[4]

In their desire to work with the Rafsanjani governments, Europe and Japan have downplayed impediments. For instance, Britain retains normal diplomatic and trade relations with Tehran despite the continuing bounty on Salman Rushdie, a prominent British citizen.[5] Similarly, Germany has not permitted the Iranian involvement in four 1992 murders in Berlin to interfere with business with Iran.

This policy of accommodation is based on the hypothesis that economic moderation—free-market policies, extensive

---

[1] *Financial Times*, November 10, 1992.

[2] Steve Coll, "German Exports Helping Iran Rebuild, Rearm," *Washington Post*, December 6, 1992.

[3] Leslie Helm, "Japan Reluctant to Back Embargo on Iran," *Washington Post*, November 14, 1992.

[4] As printed in *International Herald Tribune*, November 25, 1992.

[5] For details on how the British government worked to maintain normal ties with Iran even at the onset of the Rushdie affair in March 1989, see Daniel Pipes, *The Rushdie Affair* (New York: Birch Lane Press, 1990), pp. 33-35 and 157-159. Consider that there was no disruption in trade while Foreign Secretary Sir Geoffrey Howe assured BBC listeners on March 2, "We understand that the book itself has been found deeply offensive by people of the Muslim faith. It is a book that is offensive in many other ways as well."

trade and investment—will lead to eventual foreign policy moderation. So far, there is little evidence to support this assumption. Indeed, it could be argued that additional resources have permitted Iran to accelerate its rearmament, to step up its pressure on Gulf states, and to meddle more in Middle Eastern politics from Lebanon to Algeria and Sudan— the exact opposite of what Europe and Japan had hoped to accomplish through their policy of accommodation.

The results of this accommodationist policy appear to be similar to America's late-1980s experience with Saddam Hussein. That policy, as explained by Brent Scowcroft, "was to convince Iraq that moderate international and domestic behavior would be rewarded. [U.S. policy was] right to attempt to convince Saddam that he had more to gain from peaceful relations with the West and southern Gulf states than from confrontation, radicalism, and aggression."[1] To this end, the U.S. government provided Iraq with $1.6 billion in agricultural credits in fiscal years 1989 and 1990.[2] Washington turned a blind eye to the extension of additional loans from an Atlanta branch of an Italian bank, Banca Nazionale del Lavoro (BNL), and to the fact that Saddam was purchasing large amounts of dual-use high technology equipment in order to build a wide range of non-conventional weapons, ranging from missiles to ultra high-performance artillery, chemical weapons, and nuclear bombs.[3]

The policy of seeking to "bring Saddam into the family of nations," in President Bush's words, was a failure. Indeed, others would say it was misguided from the start. The American public, Congress, and executive branch are going to

---

[1] Brent Scowcroft, "We Didn't 'Coddle' Saddam," *Washington Post*, October 13, 1992.

[2] U.S. General Accounting Office, *Iraq's Participation in U.S. Agricultural Export Programs*, November 1990, p. 15.

[3] A detailed exposition of the Bush administration's tolerance of Iraqi actions was set forth by then Senator Albert Gore in his speech (complete with footnotes) to the Center for National Priorities on September 29, 1992. The best articulated Bush administration rebuttal of such charges was by then National Security Advisor Brent Scowcroft, "We Didn't 'Coddle' Saddam," *Washington Post*, October 13, 1992.

be reluctant to repeat a policy which required 500,000 U.S. troops to repair elsewhere in the Gulf.

It is difficult to see how a Western policy of detente with Iran will lead Tehran to abandon its perturbing aims. Perhaps the accommodationists hope that since Iran's real aim is to achieve prosperity, and since dominating the Gulf is only one means to this end, the West could offer another means of achieving the same goal, namely, access to Western technology and credits. This policy dangerously stakes a lot on a very slim hope. Two main factors work against this policy.

• *The West is unlikely to be in a position to offer Iran inducement sufficient to achieve Iran's aims.* Part of the problem is that the U.S. public and government is too suspicious of Iran's intent to agree to provide much to Iran. The 1992 White House review of policy towards Iran was on target when it concluded, in the words of the *New York Times*, "any gesture that might be politically meaningful in Tehran... would have been politically impossible at home."[1] Consider how Congress and the media approached the issue of high technology exports to Iran in the fall of 1992, while preparing for a meeting of the seven largest industrial nations (the so-called G-7) to discuss export policies toward Iran (as well as toward Libya and North Korea). The *Washington Post* ran three stories all highlighting the risks of greater trade with Iran,[2] while Congress enacted the Iran-Iraq Non-Proliferation Act of 1992. This act, which passed easily, requires the U.S. government to "urgently ... seek" the agreement of other nations—under pain of sanctions—to oppose supply to Iran of "any goods or technology, including dual-use goods or technology," which could contribute to the acquisition by Iran of unconventional weapons "or destabilizing numbers and types of advanced conventional weapons." The definition of items subject to export controls is so broad that, as one respected business

---

[1] Elaine Sciolino, *New York Times*, June 7, 1992.

[2] "U.S. Seeks to Halt Western Export of 'Dual-Use' Technology to Iran," R. Jeffrey Smith, November 10, 1992; "Technology from West Floods Iran," Steve Coll, November 10, 1992; and "U.S. Firms Buying Oil from Iran—New, Large Purchases Help Tehran to Fund Rebuilding Programs," by Steve Coll, November 8, 1992.

journal put it, it "could encompass everything developed in the computer age."[1]

But even if the U.S. were to press full steam ahead for normalization of economic ties with Iran, Iran's serious economic problems would still persist. Iran cannot, in a short time, reverse the effects of the halving of its per capita income that followed the Revolution, especially when it continues to pursue misguided policies of pouring billions into state-sponsored heavy industry.

• *Tehran's aims may well be grander than understood in the West.* If this is the case, a stronger Iran may be more, not less, interested in dominating its neighbors and in playing a major role in Middle Eastern politics. Efforts to integrate Iran into regional security structures that would allow it to advance its interests within a framework guaranteeing each state security against invasion, subversion, and coercion may well be ill-advised. Iran would be such a large presence in any regional organization that there would be a grave risk that the structure would be turned into an instrument for Iranian domination, either on its own or in conjunction with Saudi Arabia. Indeed, a GCC enlarged to include Iran would only replicate on a larger scale a problem that already plagues the GCC—the smaller states fear that the organization is so dominated by one state (either Saudi Arabia or, hypothetically, Iran) that it has become as much a threat as a protection.

The only adequate security guarantee for the Gulf states is to involve outside powers, which Tehran strongly opposes. Perhaps Iran could have become reconciled to the proposal to rely on the two most powerful Arab states, Egypt and Syria. This so-called "6+2" formula was set out in the Damascus Declaration of March 1991, immediately after Desert Storm. However, the proposal quickly became a dead letter, because the Gulf states' suspicions about Egyptian and Syrian intentions. Cairo and Damascus could use any security presence as a means to extract billions in aid. The track record of Syria in Lebanon and of Egypt in Yemen have created fears that, once stationed in the Gulf, their troops would not leave.

----

[1] Vahe Petrossian, "Iran Back in the Firing Lane," *MEED*, December 4, 1992, pp. 2-3.

Because the Gulf states are unable to trust other Middle Eastern states for their security, there is only one adequate security guarantee for the Arab states of the Gulf—the United States. Washington has already proved its willingness and ability to respond with force to repel threats to the world's largest oil reserves. The Gulf states have confidence that U.S. troops will come as soon as needed and will leave once the crisis has been resolved. Since reliance on the U.S. is, and will remain, anathema to Iran, there are few prospects that a Gulf security structure can be created that simultaneously addresses Arab needs and satisfies Iranian objections.

COMBINE CARROTS AND STICKS

For U.S. policymakers, Islamic Iran poses a quandary: at times its behavior seems to be fundamentally at cross-purposes with American interests, yet some Iranian leaders appear amenable to minimizing conflict with the U.S. One way to respond to this dilemma is through a nuanced policy of rewarding positive steps and penalizing negative actions. The U.S. could establish two distinct goalposts for Iranian behavior. If Iran passed the post on the friendly side, the U.S. would take measured positive steps. If Iran transgressed the negative goalposts, then the U.S. would respond in kind by taking negative steps.

Such a policy has many advantages: it defines the points on which the U.S. has differences with Islamic Iran, thereby demonstrating that American actions are defined by principles accepted by the community of nations rather than being motivated by a blind animus towards Islam; it allows flexibility through adjustment of the goalposts as the situation changes; it permits half steps by each side, rather than requiring an all-or-nothing approach; and it provides the public with an easily explainable framework for what could otherwise be seen as cynical *realpolitik,* or facilitating confusion.

Unfortunately, the success of a carrot-and-stick policy would be hurt by four problems.

• *Foreign governments have very limited influence on Iran,* as demonstrated by the Iran-contra debacle. The Iranian government has mastered the art of manipulating its interlocutors by telling them what they want to hear (e.g., hostages will be released) while simultaneously acting in exactly the opposite way, but disguised with a moderately credible deniability (e.g., Iranian surrogates taking new hostages). U.S. influence is further limited by the unsurprising situation that Iranian foreign policy is driven primarily by domestic imperatives, not by foreign pressures. So, for instance, Rafsanjani may decide that the least costly way to quiet internal hard-line criticism about his economic and social policy would be to support terrorists actively seeking to derail the Arab-Israeli peace process through violent means.

• *Strong emotions engendered by more than a decade of venomous relations between Iran and the U.S* may make a nuanced carrot-and-stick policy nearly impossible to carry out. The American animus towards revolutionary Iran undercuts the credibility of American carrots for Iran should it meet certain goalposts. In any event, offering carrots to Iran would be hard to explain to the American public, which bears an animus against the Islamic Republic, remembers the failure of the Iran-contra carrot policy, and, because of the Iraq experience, doubts that Middle Eastern dictators can be brought into the community of nations. On the other hand, because the U.S. has allowed Saddam Hussein to remain in power even after having sent 500,000 troops to fight against him, American threats to Tehran may not be credible. Furthermore, Iranian leaders would be reluctant to meet announced U.S. conditions, given that senior leaders generate controversy when they merely speak to a U.S. group.[1]

• *Carrots carry little weight if Iran can get the same benefits elsewhere without changing its behavior.* Iran can acquire needed finance and high technology from other advanced Western nations, though probably only from other G-7 nations since the G-7 enjoy an effective monopoly on the offshore oil and secondary recovery technologies needed to increase Iran's oil output. A carrot-and-stick policy is unlikely to work unless the Western allies can agree in advance to coordinate their responses to specific Iranian actions. This will not be easy given that Europe and Japan currently rely on a policy of accommodation. For example, as soon as the London trial over

---

[1] Cf. the episode cited above involving Iran's UN Ambassador and the Council on Foreign Relations.

the shipment of military-related machine tools to Iraq ended, the corporate successor to Matrix Churchill began to press for permission to ship $250 million of the same machine tools to Iran.[1] Even if the G-7 can overcome this hurdle, there will be a competition over which country will reap the benefits of supplying a carrot to Iran as a reward for good behavior. Each country has a commercial incentive to secure more business with Iran—a factor likely to be a major influence in those nations where, unlike the U.S., the foreign policy apparatus is sensitive to commercial interests. Iran is after all a multi-billion dollar per year market for at least four countries (Germany, Japan, France, and Italy).

Europe and Japan appear ready to dismiss American proposals that business with Iran be delayed, in part because they are sympathetic to Tehran's accusation that America will move the goalposts to keep Iran from ever realizing benefits. For years, Tehran had the impression that it stood to gain significantly if the Western hostages in Lebanon were released. "Really, the United States hasn't done anything in response to what we did in the past concerning the release of their hostages," Foreign Minister Velayati said in an interview.[2] Iranian moderates feel that they have reaped few benefits for a considerable sacrifice, in which Iran had to openly demonstrate that it was vulnerable to U.S. pressure and that it was willing to sacrifice radical Islamic principles for narrow Iranian national interests. On the other hand, U.S. diplomats argue that Tehran arranged the hostages' release precisely because the U.S. showed it would not bargain, and so that therefore the hostages brought Iran no advantage.[3]

- *The criteria for carrots and sticks will be hard to formulate.* Islamic Iran has demonstrated a remarkable talent for observing the letter of the law while violating the spirit. While Tehran has, despite bellicose public statements, been cautious

---

[1] *Financial Times*, November 20, 1992. The application was made by BSA, directed by former chairman of Matrix Churchill Keith Bailey. BSA is current owner of the Churchill lathe lines.

[2] Elaine Sciolino, "For Iran Chief, a Mandate and a Test," *New York Times*, April 14, 1992.

[3] Officials cited by Don Oberdorfer, *Washington Post*, January 20, 1992.

about crossing lines drawn in the sand it has shown a remarkable ability to find alternate paths around those lines. Consider the issue of freedom of shipping in the Gulf. The U.S. long defined the question in terms of keeping the Straits of Hormuz open. A broad consensus emerged that freedom of shipping through the Straits was a vital U.S. interest, the violation of which would bring U.S. military response. So the Iranians accomplished their aim by placing mines, not with Silkworm missiles. The result was much the same—to impede oil shipments in the Persian Gulf—but the Iranians had acted in such a way that the U.S. had difficulty organizing international support for punitive actions against Iran. The lesson from this experience should be how difficult it is to encourage good Iranian behavior by drawing a line in the sand.

In practice, the advanced industrial nations have not been able to formulate a carrot and stick policy to change Iranian behavior. Iran's nuclear power program is a good example. Iran justifies the program on the basis of undisputed power shortages and growing demand for electricity. OECD governments and international institutions are providing billions of dollars to finance Iran's power program. It should seem obvious to Washington that there should be a linkage: Iran should get less or no access to Western government loans if it presses ahead with the nuclear program, while Iran should be offered more loans on more favorable terms if it scales back or abandons its nuclear power program. To date, the U.S. has had no success in pressing its allies to make such a linkage.

A carrot-and-stick policy contains dangers that need to be carefully considered. It is likely to turn out to be less effective than hoped, and, in any case, it might not be acceptable to the American people.

CONTAINMENT

There may well be no basis for a constructive relationship between the Islamic Republic and the U.S. Basic U.S. interests may be incompatible with Tehran's drive to dominate Gulf oil, confront Turkey, gain access to the Pakistani bomb, and provide support for anti-Western Middle Eastern regimes and terrorism.

In this case, the best U.S. policy may be containment. As with the Soviet Union in decades past, this means laying down clear markers to avoid military confrontation, demonstrating a willingness to use force if those markers are crossed, and waiting for internal problems to eventually overcome the regime.

Economic weakness, and the growing disillusionment of the Iranian people with rampant corruption and continuing poverty, increase the chance that a policy of containment would succeed. Rafsanjani is quite right when he warns, "Do you think the people who have no medicine and no school, we can tell them we had a revolution and keep them busy with slogans?"[1] The reservoir of support for the clerics, once fed by the waters of hatred for the Shah, has run dry. Many remember the Shah's reign with nostalgia as a time of riches and social freedom, while those of prime rioting age are too young to have hated him (a twenty-year old in 1993 was five when the Shah left). It is quite possible that the Islamic Revolution will not last into a second generation.

A containment policy would work best if it could be coordinated with other potential suppliers of high technology to Iran. Ironically, it may be simpler to secure G-7 cooperation if Washington pushes for isolation of Iran, rather than a nuanced carrot-and-stick policy for rewarding moderate behavior. Such a principled stand could attract support in Europe; the European Community Parliament, for example, voted to suspend all commercial relations with Iran until Tehran halted human rights abuses (the Parliament can only recommend such a step; power to act rests with the European Commission).[2] Isolating Iran from international arms markets, or at least from the market in sophisticated electronic arms produced only in the West, is the area where the most coordination may be possible. The G-7 nations might be persuaded to prevent the acquisition by Iran of electronic and other upgrades that would extend the life of its aging Western weapons platforms and that would convert the Soviet-style platforms into more potent weapons.

---

[1] *Jomhuri Islami*, as printed in *Akhbaar*, December 10, 1989.

[2] *Iran Times*, June 19, 1992.

It may also be possible to isolate Iran from international capital markets because of Iran's deteriorating credit rating. The U.S. can use its influence in international institutions (such as the World Bank) and with commercial banks to insist that Iran not receive favorable treatment and that the risks of lending to Iran be assessed realistically. Banks and government credit agencies should be warned that the loans they extend are, in effect, financing Iranian armament, because the additional funds permit Iran to divert funds that would otherwise go for civilian needs for military purposes.

The willingness to use force when the containing walls are breached must be built into containment. The U.S. needs to spell out its vital interests in the region frequently in presidential statements, repeated *ad nauseam* by U.S. diplomats on all appropriate occasions. Two basic points that need to be drummed into Iranian observers are the security of all Gulf states from coercion and the security of Turkey from overt or implicit threats to its vital interests. Such statements may have limited effect, but if they give Tehran cause to pause and reflect, then the effort will be worthwhile. In the end, however, the U.S. must be prepared to demonstrate its commitment to these interests through its willingness to use force.

A containment policy toward Iran is unlikely to require Desert Storm II. The challenge from Iran will probably be more subtle, such as an escalation of pressure on the smaller Gulf states to exclude the U.S. from the region or to cede income to Iran through mechanisms such as a larger quota for Iranian oil or joint ventures in which the Arab partner receives no benefit. The U.S. will need to support its allies vigorously and promptly dozens of times when they face real but limited threats; thus, a containment policy toward Iran will not require the deployment of a half million American troops, as was the case with Iraq.

EVALUATING THE CHARACTER OF THE IRANIAN CHALLENGE

The challenge to the West from Iran should not be exaggerated. Iran is not a superpower. No matter how bitterly it opposes the West, it is not a credible threat to Western hegemony. The most potent challenge Iran could pose would be if it were able to form an alliance that stretched from a

fundamentalist North Africa through a rejectionist Syria and
an Iranian-influenced Arabian Peninsula to Iran and on to
nuclear Pakistan, with ties to China. Such an alliance would be
a major setback to the West, but the West could learn to live
with even this unlikely possibility under certain conditions. If
the cold peace between Israel and its Arab neighbors persisted,
if oil continued to flow from the Persian Gulf at a reasonable
price, if weapons of mass destruction did not pose an
unacceptable threat to outside states, and if international
terrorism received essentially no Iranian support, then the
West would be unlikely to use force against an Iranian
alliance.

Nevertheless, the U.S. government must prepare for the
possibility that Iran will challenge vital Western interests. The
present Iranian government does seem bent on posing a
challenge to the West on several fronts: on Arab-Israeli peace,
on the flow of oil at a reasonable price, on weapons of mass
destruction, and on terrorism. It would be an error to assume
that a deal can be struck with Tehran on any one of these
issues without resolving the others, for that would only free
Iran to concentrate on challenging the West on another front.
Tehran's broadsides against the West require equally broad
responses.

In order to contain Iran and restore the balance of power in
the Gulf, Egypt and other regional actors have argued that the
West should ease up on sanctions toward Iraq, Iran's natural
enemy. This is an unnecessary and dangerous step, however.
Iran can be contained largely through the denial of loans and
high technology combined with a credible Western threat to
retaliate for Iranian terrorism and subversion. If the U.S. were
to ease up on Iraq and allow it to rebuild, there is a risk that both
Tehran and Baghdad will see this as a signal of a reduced
American commitment to the protection of its Gulf allies.
Though unlikely, it is possible that in such a case Iran and Iraq
would begin to cooperate on the basis of their common hatred
of the West and their desire to expand oil revenue at the
expense of Saudi Arabia. An anti-Western Iran-Iraq alliance
aimed at dominating the Gulf could form regardless of
whether Saddam remains in power. Iran has signaled its
willingness to work with Iraq with either Saddam or a
Saddam-clone. Rafsanjani said on January 31, 1993 that,
although he would prefer a "popular government" in Iraq, he

would be prepared to cooperate with the present Iraqi government under certain conditions.[1] Although it is unlikely, a Baghdad-Tehran pact would be a profound threat to America's interest in guaranteeing the free flow of oil. The U.S. should thus seek to maintain UN sanctions against Iraq to prevent this scenario from coming into being. In any case, Iran can be contained without having to rebuild Iraq.

It might seem logical for Iran to bide its time before mounting its challenge the West. After all, in a few years, Iran will have acquired a variety of weapon systems, possibly including nuclear weapons, while the U.S. will have cut the size of its forces. However, Tehran does not appear to share this perception; it is acting as if the time to strike is the present. Perhaps Iran's leaders feel that this is a particularly propitious moment because of an upsurge of Islamic fervor and the disarray in the wake of the Soviet Union's dissolution and Iraq's defeat, while delay would be dangerous because it would allow the Arab states of the Gulf to acquire more weapons and Israel to reach peace with its Arab neighbors. Whatever the calculations, Tehran seems to be moving on a swift time schedule. It would be an error to assume that there will not be a major Iranian challenge in the short term.

---

[1] *Mideast Mirror*, February 1, 1993. The conditions were worded in such a way that they could be either minor or insuperable obstacles. Rafsanjani said that he was willing to return the Iraqi planes that flew to Iran for sanctuary during the Gulf War as soon as the UN authorized such an exemptions to the sanctions against Iraq.

RECENT PUBLICATIONS OF THE WASHINGTON INSTITUTE

Towards a New Era in U.S.-Israel Relations—Proceedings of The Washington Institute's Seventh Annual Policy Conference

A Tunisian View of the New Middle East—Proceedings of Statesman Series speech by Foreign Minister of Tunisia Habib Ben Yahia

Pursuing Peace: An American Strategy for the Arab-Israeli Peace Process—The final report of The Washington Institute's Strategic Study Group, with recommendations for U.S. policy in the peace negotiations by a distinguished group of Middle East experts including Samuel Lewis, Michael Mandelbaum, Peter Rodman and Martin Indyk

Democracy and Arab Political Culture—A Washington Institute Monograph by Elie Kedourie

Security for Peace: Israel's Minimal Security Requirements in Negotiations with the Palestinians by Ze'ev Schiff

POLICY PAPERS SERIES

Policy Paper 32: *"The Arab Street"?: Public Opinion in the Arab World* by David Pollock

Policy Paper 31: *Arming for Peace? Syria's Elusive Quest for "Strategic Parity"* by Michael Eisenstadt

Policy Paper 30: *The Economic Consequences of the Persian Gulf War: Accelerating Opec's Demise* by Eliyahu Kanovsky

Policy Paper 29: *King Hussein's Strategy of Survival* by Uriel Dann

Policy Paper 28: *The Arrow Next Time?: Israel's Missile Defense Program for the 1990s* by Marvin Feuerwerger

Policy Paper 27: *Palestinian Self-Government (Autonomy): Its Past and its Future* by Harvey Sicherman

Policy Paper 26: *Damascus Courts the West: Syrian Politics, 1989-1991* by Daniel Pipes

Policy Paper 25: *Economic Consequences of Peace for Israel, the Palestinians, and Jordan* by Patrick L. Clawson and Howard Rosen

Policy Paper 24: *The Future of Iraq* by Laurie Mylroie

POLICY FOCUS SERIES

Policy Focus 20: *Water and the Peace Process: Two Perspectives* by Shlomo Gur (Israel) and Munther Haddadin (Jordan)

Policy Focus 19: *Hamas: The Fundamentalist Challenge to the PLO* by Clinton Bailey

Policy Focus 18: *Baghdad Between Shi'a and Kurds* by Ofra Bengio

For a complete listing or to order publications, write or call The Washington Institute for Near East Policy, 1828 L Street, NW, Suite 1050, Washington, D.C. 20036 Phone (202) 452-0650, Fax (202) 223-5364